FOCUSED FOR FASTPITCH

Gloria Solomon, PhD
and
Andrea Becker

Human Kinetics

Library of Congress Cataloging-in-Publication Data

Solomon, Gloria, 1959-
  Focused for fastpitch / Gloria Solomon and Andrea Becker.
    p. cm.
Includes bibliographical references.
  ISBN 0-7360-5084-1 (soft cover)
  1. Softball--Training. 2. Softball--Coaching. I. Becker, Andrea,
1978- II. Title.
  GV881.4.T72S65 2004
  796.357'8--dc22

2003027575

ISBN: 0-7360-5084-1

Acquisitions Editor: Jana Hunter; **Managing Editor:** Wendy McLaughlin; **Assistant Editor:** Kim Thoren; **Copyeditor:** Pat Connelly; **Proofreader:** Coree Clark; **Permission Manager:** Toni Harte; **Graphic Designer:** Nancy Rasmus; **Graphic Artist:** Tara Welsch; **Photo Manager:** Dan Wendt; **Cover Designer:** Keith Blomberg; **Photographer (cover):** ©Sportschrome; **Photographer (interior):** Human Kinetics, unless otherwise noted; **Art Manager:** Kareema McLendon; **Illustrator:** Brian McElwain; **Printer:** Versa Press

Human Kinetics books are available at special discounts for bulk purchase. Special editions or book excerpts can also be created to specification. For details, contact the Special Sales Manager at Human Kinetics.

Printed in the United States of America   10 9 8 7 6 5 4 3 2 1

Human Kinetics
Web site: www.HumanKinetics.com

United States: Human Kinetics
P.O. Box 5076
Champaign, IL 61825-5076
800-747-4457
e-mail: humank@hkusa.com

Canada: Human Kinetics
475 Devonshire Road Unit 100
Windsor, ON N8Y 2L5
800-465-7301 (in Canada only)
e-mail: orders@hkcanada.com

Europe: Human Kinetics
107 Bradford Road
Stanningley
Leeds LS28 6AT, United Kingdom
+44 (0) 113 255 5665
e-mail: hk@hkeurope.com

Australia: Human Kinetics
57A Price Avenue
Lower Mitcham, South Australia 5062
08 8277 1555
e-mail: liaw@hkaustralia.com

New Zealand: Human Kinetics
Division of Sports Distributors NZ Ltd.
P.O. Box 300 226 Albany
North Shore City
Auckland
0064 9 448 1207
e-mail: blairc@hknewz.com

FOCUSED FOR FASTPITCH

CONTENTS

1 Mentaphysical Training   **1**

Train the mind to improve the body's
performance.

2 Thinking the Game   **23**

Utilize constructive attitudes and routines
to gain the edge.

3 Hitting   **45**

Relax and regroup to stay in the zone.

4 Bunting   **77**

Execute the short game with patience
and precision.

FOREWORD

Have you ever told one of your players, "Just relax and hit the ball"? I'll bet you've trained your athletes on the mechanics of swinging a bat, but have you ever taught them how to relax? Have you spent much time teaching your players how to manage their energy levels? Ever wondered what you could have done to prevent your team from playing flat, devoid of the proper emotional energy or arousal level needed to be successful?

Developing softball players into competitive athletes is about so much more than just physically working hard at practice. There is a huge mental component that needs to be addressed as well. Mental toughness, concentration, mental imagery, and a healthy mental approach to the rigors of daily practice are skills that need to be taught to ensure the success and well-being of the players.

The softball team at Sacramento State meets weekly with our sport psychology consultant to learn mental skills and how to use them to enhance physical performance. One of my roles on the softball field is to help the athletes incorporate these mental skills into practice and game situations. The drills in this book allow my staff and me to hone in on the mental skills of my players in practice. For instance, there are several hitting drills that teach players how to regulate their energy levels in the batter's box. While the players work on improving their hitting technique, they are also practicing breathing exercises, performance routines, or other strategies to improve their mental game—developing into more complete athletes by using specific mental skills to enhance their physical performance. Ultimately, my goal is to get the players to be able to incorporate these strategies into their actual game performance so that they are maximally prepared for any challenges that may arise during competition.

Although many coaches recognize the need to develop mental skills, few are willing to give up time in practice to do so. Now, thanks to authors Gloria Solomon and Andrea Becker, you don't have to. With the drills you'll find in *Focused for Fastpitch*, your players will be practicing mental and physical skills simultaneously. Not only will you maximize your practice time, but your players will make vast improvements on the field.

**Kathy Strahan, head softball coach,
California State University at Sacramento**

ACKNOWLEDGMENTS

When the idea for this book came about, we had no concept of the work and commitment involved in such a project. Almost two years after its inception, this book is now ready to share with you, the reader. We would like to publicly acknowledge those people who contributed to our endeavor. Among those who gave freely of their ideas, wisdom, and editorial assistance are Dr. Becky Sisley, who provided guidance at the beginning by critiquing our original proposal; Coach Kathy Strahan, who read over several of the drills and provided thoughtful critiques; Coach Gene Vigil, who got his athletes together and allowed us to test out our drills on the practice field; the 10 coaches who agreed to share their favorite drills with us; and to the editors at Human Kinetics for putting it all together.

INTRODUCTION

There is ample evidence suggesting a link between an athlete's mental state and physical performance. The connection between mind and body has particular significance in performance settings that involve precision and expertise. Consider the types of mental training and testing required for those people in such professions as airline pilot or surgeon. These professionals must perform precise, high-risk physical movements. The mental discipline required for such expert performance is profound. Similarly, competitive athletes who are expected to perform precise and expert movements also benefit from mental training. Recently, serious athletes have gone beyond focusing solely on physical skill development; they now apply principles of mechanics, nutrition, and conditioning to get the competitive edge on opponents. However, mental training is often neglected. In fact, most softball books for the coach and player ignore mental training altogether.

Coaches and athletes in every sport, from badminton to football, agree that the mental components of competition play a significant role in performance. On a daily basis, coaches directly and indirectly address mental skills such as motivation and concentration. However, many coaches assume that athletes can acquire and develop mental skills without practice. How often have you heard a coach say "just relax" to a batter at the plate with two outs and runners in scoring position? In order to handle the pressure of batting, or perform any skill in a crucial situation, an athlete must be mentally prepared and have the ability to cope with competitive pressure. Although coaches and athletes rave about the importance of "mental toughness" in sport, minimal attention is devoted to the training of mental skills.

Learning to integrate psychological skills into practice does not require specialized training. *Mentaphysical* training, the method introduced in this book, allows coaches and players to develop the mental game on the field. Mentaphysical training is a new approach to coaching that teaches physical and mental skills simultaneously.

This method requires that players learn and practice mental skills while cultivating and refining the physical skills through specially designed drills. These drills target the physical components of softball—such as hitting, pitching, and fielding—and also address the specific mental factors identified as important in the sport of softball.

The purpose of this book is to provide coaches and players with drills that integrate physical and mental skills. This book serves as a practical guide for implementing these unique drills into any competitive fastpitch softball practice, including high school and college settings. Mental training techniques are incorporated directly into practice sessions. All too often, coaches plead for players to "focus" while in the batter's box, yet it is the rare coach who has taught those players how to practice the skill of concentration while hitting. Why not take the opportunity, with mentaphysical drills, to teach athletes *how* to focus while refining their softball skills?

Chapter 1 introduces the concept of mentaphysical training and the four major mental factors included in the drills: energy regulation, concentration, confidence, and mental imagery. Methods are provided for measuring, regulating, and evaluating these four factors, including worksheets, questionnaires, and scorecards. Chapter 2 sets the foundation for thinking your way through the game by using the principles of performance excellence. Chapters 3 through 9 contain mentaphysical drills that focus on the individual aspects of each position: hitting, bunting, baserunning, infield and outfield defense, pitching, and catching. These chapters also include drills from top coaches such as Jacquie Joseph, Connie Clark, and John Reeves. Chapter 10 discusses team play and how to build your team up mentally as well as physically through cohesion, role definition, and communication.

This book is designed for the committed softball coach and player. By adopting a new way of thinking about softball drills and using mentaphysical training, coaches and players will no longer have to guess how to relax or ponder how to stay focused. By incorporating mental and physical skills together, players will be at their best in the heat of competition.

DRILL FINDER

KEY TO DIAGRAMS

1B	first baseman
2B	second baseman
3B	third baseman
C/CO	coach
C1	coach 1
C2	coach 2
F	feeder
X	fielder
SS	shortstop

ADDITIONAL EQUIPMENT FOR DRILLS

All drills require the use of standard softball equipment. Some drills may call for additional equipment as listed below.

bucket or garbage can

cones

foam softballs

full-length mirror

hitting screen (sock)

hitting tee

pitching machine

rope

stopwatch

striped softballs

targets

weighted softballs

Mentaphysical Training

Softball players practice their sport for several hours a week, and some players even practice three to four hours a day. During this practice time, most players and coaches concentrate solely on improving physical skills and techniques. Although physical repetition is necessary for players to improve their abilities, in order to consistently perform well, they must also practice the mental skills which will facilitate the development of each physical skill.

For example, coaches often want their players to be disciplined in the batter's box. To be a disciplined hitter, a player must use a combination of both mental and physical skills. Good hand–eye coordination, quick reaction time, and correct technique for swinging the bat are physical skills needed for hitting; however, to be a successful hitter, a player must also master the mental aspects of hitting such as knowing the count, recognizing the type of pitch, and only swinging at good pitches. Because the mind is what triggers physical action, in order to discipline the body, players must also discipline the mind. This holds true not only for hitting but for all types of physical skills. Therefore, mentaphysical training, a method that enables players to practice mental and physical skills simultaneously, is the best way to enhance overall softball performance.

Using a mentaphysical training approach will not only help players deal with situations in the game of softball but will also provide them with strategies that can be used in the game of life. This book is designed to help players and coaches incorporate mentaphysical training into practice. The drills presented in this book (chapters 3 through 9) combine strategies to improve mental skills—including energy regulation, concentration, confidence, and mental imagery—while practicing the physical skills needed for each aspect of the game.

ENERGY REGULATION

Energy regulation is the most important mental skill needed to consistently perform well at elite levels of competition. The concept of energy regulation refers to the body's physical and psychological activating systems. A person's energy level is constantly fluctuating throughout the day and can range from intense excitement to deep sleep. A person may experience high or low levels of energy at any given time depending on a variety of circumstances. Performing different skills will require different levels of energy. For example, putting a golf ball does not require the same amount of energy as teeing off. Therefore, when an athlete is expected to perform, the ability to modify and regulate energy becomes crucial. A player cannot expect to play at her best if she is not operating at the most appropriate energy level for the task at hand.

The optimal energy level will depend on two things: a player's individual preference and the type of task. When asked, "What is your energy like when you are performing well?" most players will have a definite answer such as "really high" or "pretty low." A player's response to this question represents her personal preference, which may vary depending on the demands of specified tasks. For example, a shortstop who generally prefers to be calm and relaxed when she is playing defense may need to get "pumped up," or increase her energy, to perform her best in the batter's box. A player's preferred energy level for a specific skill must match the actual energy level she experiences when performing that skill. If this shortstop needs to be pumped up in order to hit well, she must adjust her energy when transitioning from defense to offense. Thus, it is a great asset for players to be able to recognize and then regulate energy levels according to their personal preference and the demands of a specific type of task.

Just as coaches and players monitor physical improvements in sport, they should also monitor mental progress. Unfortunately, mental progress is much more difficult to measure on a daily basis. In order to determine and track fluctuations in energy, a point of reference must first be established. When does the player perform her best? What is her optimal energy level for maximum performance? Answering the questions provided in figure 1.1 will help a player determine her preferred energy level.

Energy Problems

When a player is not performing at her optimal energy level, several problems may ensue. The inability to regulate energy can negatively affect a player's concentration and confidence. Muscle tension is one of the most common side effects of improper energy regulation. If a hitter is at the plate with two strikes, during a tie game, with a runner on third base, her body may become tense. When muscles tighten, it is difficult to coordinate movements with efficiency. Thus, the hitter will have a slower reaction time and jerky movements when she swings the bat. This will make it more difficult for her to make solid contact with the ball. If the hitter fails

Figure 1.1 Determining Your Preferred Energy Level

Instructions: Take some time to reflect on where your energy level is when you are playing softball. Think about your needs when you are performing in games and in practice on both offense and defense, and respond to the following questions.

1. Are there times during your performance when having increased levels of energy is important? If yes, when are those times?

2. Are there times during your performance when having lower levels of energy is important? If yes, when are those times?

3. Think about the last time you had a great performance (offensively or defensively). What was your energy level during this performance? Did it change depending on the demands of the situation (batting versus defending)?

4. Think about the last time you had a poor performance. What was your energy level during this performance? What were your thoughts and feelings focused on during this performance?

5. On the continuum below, mark the point (with an O) where you think your energy level needs to be for you to perform your best on offense. Then mark another point (with an X) where you think your energy level needs to be for you to perform your best on defense. Reflect on successful experiences and your answers to the questions above to help you identify these levels. Then explain why you believe these are the best energy levels for optimal performance.

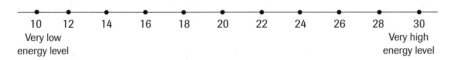

| 10 | 12 | 14 | 16 | 18 | 20 | 22 | 24 | 26 | 28 | 30 |

Very low
energy level

Very high
energy level

Explanation: Scores for both offense and defense will range from 10 to 30. Scores between 10 to 16 = low energy, 17 to 23 = moderate energy, and 24 to 30 = high energy.

4

to execute in this situation, she is likely to try even harder during her next at-bat. Often, when players are not performing well, they think that trying harder will solve the problem. Unfortunately, this extra effort continues to increase energy and muscle tension, and it rarely leads to success.

A player who is experiencing muscle tension may also find it difficult to direct her attention to relevant details of the game, such as keeping her eye on the ball. Although she may believe she is putting forth her best effort, this hitter is likely to strike out or make lousy contact with the ball. Continued failure caused by muscle tension or by decreases in concentration will undermine the player's confidence. Frustrated with her performance, she will likely question her hitting ability. At this point, it is common to hear a player say, "I just can't do it" or "What am I doing wrong?" Unfortunately, the player may even want to change her hitting mechanics, believing the problem has to do with technique when it is really a problem with energy regulation. Therefore, players must be able to recognize and regulate their energy because improper levels of energy are likely to increase muscle tension. This can decrease concentration and confidence and subsequently decrease overall performance.

There are numerous mental and physical qualities associated with energy levels. The Energy Level Evaluation worksheet (see figure 1.2) enables players to measure their energy level based on how they felt during a game or practice. Players can complete this form to measure their energy level at practice, during specific drills, or in actual games. Performance excellence is achieved when a player's actual energy level (figure 1.2) matches her preferred energy level (figure 1.1).

Decreasing Energy Level

When a player faces a pressure situation, experiences failure, or is overly excited, she is likely to have feelings of anxiousness, fear, or frustration. These types of emotional changes can cause undue increases in energy that are detrimental to performance. Softball players often carry their momentum from offense to defense or from defense to offense. A hitter who is upset after striking out or making the last out of the inning may carry an increased level of energy and frustration onto the field as she takes her defensive position. If this player does not perform well at a higher energy level while playing defense, she is more likely to perform poorly

Figure 1.2 Energy Level Evaluation

Instructions: This evaluation should be implemented directly after practice or competition. Evaluate your energy level by identifying how you felt when performing on either offense or defense. Select a number (1, 2, or 3) for each word listed below to indicate whether that word describes how you felt.

Today in practice or competition, I felt the following:

	True	Somewhat true	Not true
High Energy			
Excited	3	2	1
Butterflies	3	2	1
Intense	3	2	1
Energized	3	2	1
Activated	3	2	1
Low Energy			
Calm	1	2	3
Composed	1	2	3
Loose	1	2	3
Relaxed	1	2	3
Tranquil	1	2	3

Total the scores for each section to rate your energy level during practice or competition. Complete the survey twice to determine your actual energy levels for both offense and defense, then record your scores below.

Scores for both offense and defense will range from 10 to 30. Scores of 10 to 16 = low energy, 17 to 23 = moderate energy, 24 to 30 = high energy.

Energy level score for offense: _____

Energy level score for defense: _____

To evaluate your ability to regulate your energy levels, compare your preferred energy levels for offense and defense (identified in figure 1.1) to the actual energy levels experienced during practice or competition. For comparisons, scores from figures 1.1 and 1.2 can be plotted on the continuum below.

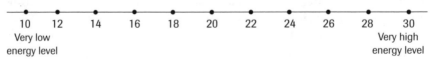

| 10 | 12 | 14 | 16 | 18 | 20 | 22 | 24 | 26 | 28 | 30 |

Very low
energy level

Very high
energy level

Are your actual energy levels for offense and defense above or below your preferred energy levels? If so, refer to the energy regulation strategies for increasing and decreasing energy (outlined in chapter 1).

and may even commit an error. This describes a situation in which a negative outcome led to increases in energy, but positive outcomes can also increase energy. For example, a fielder who makes a great play for the third out of an inning may bring her excitement into the dugout. If she is the leadoff batter for that inning, her excitement may make it difficult for her to calm down and prepare to hit. Regardless of whether the outcome is positive or negative, players must be able to adjust their energy in preparation for the next task. This is why coaches often tell their players to relax when performing a skill.

To help players learn to decrease their energy level to an optimal level for performance, several energy-decreasing strategies are woven into the drills presented in this book. These calming techniques include simple breathing exercises, acute relaxation responses, calming cue words, and pre-performance routines.

Here are some examples of techniques players can use to reduce their energy level:

• **Rhythmic breathing.** The player inhales slowly, counting to four (1-2-3-4), and then exhales slowly, counting down from four (4-3-2-1). She then pauses for a count of four (1-2-3-4). She repeats the sequence two to four times.

• **Thought control.** The player identifies thoughts that are causing overarousal. She controls these thoughts by telling herself that she needs to reduce her energy level. She uses a cue word or statement to reduce her arousal.

• **Storing extra energy.** The player acknowledges that she has extra energy, and she "stores" that energy in her energy bank. She knows that it will be there to use when needed.

• **Deactivating cues.** The player decreases her energy level by saying a short word or phrase to calm herself (for example, "relax," "cool down," or "loose and easy").

• **Mind music.** The player decreases her energy by "playing" or "singing" a relaxing song in her mind. She keeps this song handy for use when needed.

Increasing Energy Level

Just as a player must be able to decrease her energy, she must also be able to increase her energy. Before a game begins, players are typically transitioning from a resting mode to a playing mode.

The transition often requires players to increase their energy in order to get to an optimal level for performance. They do this by warming up before they play; players who do not warm up properly may still be feeling a little flat or timid when play begins, which may lead to a lazy attitude and a lack of concentration. This may explain why breakdowns in performance often occur during the first few innings of play.

Another instance when a player may need to increase her energy is when she is feeling tired or fatigued during competition. This is common in tournaments when teams are playing three or more games in one day. Fortunately, there are ways to prevent the problems that arise from low levels of energy. This book includes drills that are designed to allow players to practice energy-increasing methods such as intense breathing, exaggerated movements, cue words, and pre-performance routines.

Here are some examples of the techniques players can use to increase their energy level:

• **Burst of energy.** The player increases her energy level by performing a vigorous activity (for example, performing high knee lifts in place for 10 seconds). This will increase her heart rate and activate her physical and mental systems.

• **Activating cues.** The player increases her energy level by using a short word or phrase to gear up for performing (for example, "hustle," "go for it," "charge up," "psych up," or "ready go").

• **Control what you can.** The player identifies and directs her attention to one thing about her energy level that she can control (for example, her mental focus on the requirements of an activity or her positive statements about performing).

• **Complete exhalation.** The player inhales naturally and holds it for 10 seconds. She feels the tension in her lungs and chest as she holds her breath. She then exhales vigorously, releasing the built-up tension. She repeats this sequence five times.

• **Mind music.** The player increases her energy by "playing" or "singing" an upbeat song in her mind. She keeps this song handy for use when needed.

Players should use figure 1.3 to chart their energy level progress.

Figure 1.3   Monitoring Energy Levels

Instructions: Specify your preferred energy levels for offense and defense as recorded in figure 1.1. Use the following table to track your energy levels and performance for each practice and game.

Preferred energy levels

Date	Context	Energy level— offense	Energy level— defense	Performance notes	Rating 1 = Low 10 = High
Month/ day/year	Practice	13	14	Felt tired today; didn't get enough sleep last night	4

Offense: _____   Defense: _____

- Date: Enter the date on which the practice or game occurred (mm/dd/yy).
- Context: Indicate whether this entry is for a practice or game.
- Energy levels: Enter your actual energy levels for offense and defense as determined using figure 1.2.
- Performance notes: Describe how you felt and explain your energy level score.
- Rating: Rate your overall performance during the practice or game.

Compare your actual energy levels with your preferred energy levels to determine which strategies to implement to consistently achieve optimal performance.

CONCENTRATION

When a player can effectively regulate her energy, she will be able to achieve a mental state that allows her to concentrate better. Simply put, concentration refers to the ability to pay attention to factors that are relevant to the immediate game situation (for example, the number of outs, the score, the coach's signals, how the defense is positioned, and environmental conditions). Players must be able to completely focus and shift their attention when appropriate. Effective concentration depends on two factors: a player's dominant attention style and the demands of the specific task. Dominant attention style refers to the type of focus a player uses most of the time. A player's dominant style may be internal (she focuses on factors within herself, such as her own thoughts) or external (she focuses on factors outside of herself, such as the actions of others). Furthermore, a player's internal or external focus may be broad, which means she is paying attention to many things, or narrow, which means she is only paying attention to one or two things.

To improve their concentration skills, players must be able to recognize their dominant attention style and shift that style according to the nature of the task. For example, an outfielder who uses a broad external attention style when she is fielding must be able to shift to a narrow attention style when she is up to bat. This will allow her to concentrate solely on the ball, increasing her chances of getting a hit. If she continues to use her dominant style and is unable to shift her attention appropriately, she will be distracted by irrelevant cues and will have difficulty making solid contact at the plate. The drills in this book allow players to explore the various attention styles, identify their dominant style, and learn to recognize and shift attention on command.

When players encounter pressure situations, regardless of the task, they will revert to their dominant attention style. If their dominant style does not meet the demands of the specified task, they are not likely to achieve the desired results. Developing an awareness of the different attention styles will help players shift to the most appropriate style for the current situation. Players can use figure 1.4 to help determine their dominant style of concentration.

A player must also be able to turn her focus on and off when needed. It is virtually impossible to concentrate for extended peri-

Figure 1.4   Concentration Assessment Form

Instructions: Read the following statement about how you focus your attention. Complete the sentence below by circling the number that represents how you usually respond in game situations.

In highly interactive situations, such as when multiple runners are advancing and the ball is in play, I am more likely to:

1. focus on everything that is occurring around me
2. focus on my thoughts about the situation
3. focus on one aspect of the situation occurring around me
4. focus on one thing I need to do and how I will get it done

Scoring:

If you chose statement #1, your predominant attention style is Broad External (BE).

If you chose statement #2, your predominant attention style is Broad Internal (BI).

If you chose statement #3, your predominant attention style is Narrow External (NE).

If you chose statement #4, your predominant attention style is Narrow Internal (NI).

Dominant attention style: _____

ods. The ability to take "microbreaks" in a manner that corresponds with the pace of the game will allow the player to concentrate more effectively and efficiently.

Concentration Problems

Softball is a sport with a lot of "downtime." Therefore, it invites many opportunities for players to get distracted. During the course of a game, a player's attention may be diverted to factors that are not relevant to the immediate game situation. For example, if a defensive player makes an error and continues to dwell on her mistake, she will have difficulty focusing on the next play. Other factors that may distract players include weather conditions, the fans, bad calls, and fatigue. With all these possible distractions, a player will benefit greatly if she is able to adjust and redirect her attention on command. If concentration is interrupted, and the player is unable to refocus her attention promptly, she cannot expect to achieve a high level of performance. Disturbances in focus can turn a consistent performer into an erratic one.

Enhancing Concentration

After a player identifies her dominant attention style and learns how to shift back and forth between styles, she should begin to note which style is appropriate for specific situations within the game. For example, hitting a ball requires a narrow external attention style, whereas reading the defense requires a broad external attention style.

Players will use more than one attention style for the execution of some skills. For each at-bat, a hitter may first use a broad external attention style to read the situation and pick up signs from her coach. She may then focus her attention internally to process the information and make a decision about what she is going to do. Finally, she will shift to a narrow external style in which she is directing all of her attention to seeing the ball. To determine the most appropriate attention style to meet the demands of a given situation, a player must identify which environmental cues are relevant (for example, the pitcher's release point). This information will allow the player to know which style to use and when to switch between styles while performing a skill. The drills in this book are designed to teach and enhance concentration through the use of cue words, attention shifting, and pre-performance routines. When there are breaks in the action, which is a common occurrence in the sport of softball, pre-performance routines are the most effective way to sustain concentration. Figure 1.5 will help players chart their ability to concentrate in varied situations.

CONFIDENCE

Confidence is not just a player's belief in her ability to hit the ball or field a grounder; it is her overall belief that she can accomplish anything she desires both on and off the softball diamond. Simply stated, confidence is about expecting to be successful. It is the personal belief that you can perform a task competently. Confidence is the critical factor that separates successful players from the rest. Successful athletes consistently report higher levels of confidence than their less successful competitors. Although confidence may seem like an intangible aspect of a player's personality, it should be thought of as a skill that can be learned, strengthened, and applied in competition. Developing confidence involves experiencing success and thinking positively. Figure 1.6 will help players assess their level of confidence.

Figure 1.5 Concentration Evaluation

Instructions: Rate your ability to concentrate during the following softball scenarios by circling the number that represents your ability to focus in that situation.

	Focus is weak; attention distracted	Sometimes focused; sometimes distracted		Very focused on relevant cues	
1. Stepping into the batter's box	1	2	3	4	5
2. Preparing to lay down a bunt	1	2	3	4	5
3. Stealing a base	1	2	3	4	5
4. Fielding a ground ball	1	2	3	4	5
5. Fielding a bunt	1	2	3	4	5
6. Fielding a deep fly ball	1	2	3	4	5
7. Turning a double play	1	2	3	4	5
8. Catching a pop-up	1	2	3	4	5

Coaching Tip: Use these situations or create additional ones. Customize the items for each player. For example, "fielding a bunt" will only be relevant for infielders and not for outfielders.

Interpretation: If the player rates her focus as a 3 or below, this is an indication that she could benefit from concentration training for that specific situation.

Figure 1.6 Confidence Assessment Form

Instructions: Confident players display their beliefs in a number of ways. The following is a list of the characteristics of confident players. Rate yourself on these characteristics.

During practice and competition, I am generally. . .

	Not True	Somewhat true	True
Positive	1	2	3
Focused	1	2	3
Goal directed	1	2	3
Motivated	1	2	3
Aggressive	1	2	3
Intense	1	2	3
Resilient	1	2	3
Disciplined	1	2	3
Composed	1	2	3
Self-controlled	1	2	3

Confidence score: _____ (Range 10-30)

Scores of 10 to 15 = low confidence, 16 to 24 = moderate confidence, 25 to 30 = high confidence.

Confidence Problems

The opposite of confidence is self-doubt. If a player experiences even the slightest tinge of self-doubt, she will not be able to perform up to her full potential. Achieving success requires taking risks, but players who lack confidence play very conservatively. They are usually not playing to win. Instead, they are playing not to lose or not to make a mistake. If a player is battling with self-doubt, her true opponent will not matter because her own self-doubt will win every time.

Confidence can be seen in a player's eyes and body language. When a player lacks confidence, it is obvious to others, especially opponents. Players who lack confidence will avoid eye contact, hurry through the motions, and appear as though they are already defeated. They may drag their feet, hang their head, or exhibit a

One of the most important psychological traits for a pitcher to possess is confidence; without it, you can't control the game.

slumped body posture. When players show signs of low confidence, it is like a personal invitation for their opponents to pounce on them. Not only does it help the opponent, but it also reinforces their own negative thinking, which leads to negative consequences. Players who lack confidence use phrases such as "I hope I don't make a mistake," which often translates into an error, or "I never get a hit against this pitcher," which often translates into a strikeout. Since the mind tells the body what to do, if the mind tells the body that it can't do something, then the body is not likely to do it. If a player believes that she does not have the ability to perform successfully against a certain team or at a given position, that belief will become a self-fulfilling prophecy and limit her performance potential. When a player lacks confidence, she may lose motivation, suffer from fear and anxiety, and have improper focus. A low level of confidence also makes a player more susceptible to problems with energy regulation. When a player is not confident in a certain situation, she is likely to become anxious or nervous. As mentioned earlier, this is a trigger for increased muscle tension.

Players who lack confidence are more likely to personalize comments made by the coaching staff. For example, if a coach is talking to an entire team about swinging at better pitches, one player may automatically think the coach is talking directly to her (even if she hit well that day). Players with low confidence ask a lot of questions about their performance, such as "Is this right?" "How do I look?" or "What am I doing wrong?" These players will often make excuses or give explanations for why they performed a certain way. If the coach does offer corrective feedback, this player is likely to think that the coach corrected her because the coach feels she is not good enough. In contrast, a confident player will use corrective instruction by her coach as information to change her actions and will not question what the coach is thinking. After making an error, a player who lacks confidence may question her ability and doubt that she is good enough; this type of player needs a lot of support and reinforcement. A confident player knows she has the ability to consistently perform well and does not dwell on errors; she knows she is good and does not need to be told or reminded.

The behaviors and actions of a player with low confidence can negatively influence an entire team. When the going gets tough, these players are the first to give up or express negative thoughts about the situation. These players often exhibit negative attitudes about themselves and also about their teammates. If a negative attitude is not addressed, it can spread like a disease that eats away at the team's chemistry and overall performance.

Enhancing Confidence

Like all learned skills, confidence can be improved. This book includes offensive and defensive drills that emphasize four strategies for enhancing confidence: performance success, composure, self-talk, and positive affirmations. The best way for a player to build confidence is to experience success. When a player sees positive results, she will feel good about herself. A player who feels good about herself and her performance will demonstrate a positive, composed, and confident demeanor. This will serve to facilitate a high level of confidence during practice and competition. Self-talk and positive affirmations are additional strategies used in the drills to encourage confident thinking.

Self-Talk

Self-talk is simply the inner conversations that people have with themselves (with conscious or unconscious awareness). This internal dialogue can be constructive or destructive depending on the content of a person's thoughts. Self-talk is extremely important because what a person says to herself represents how she thinks about herself. In addition, her thoughts influence her actions. So if a player tells herself that she is not a good hitter, then she will not become a good hitter. If a player tells herself that she is a great hitter and can hit anything, she is more likely to succeed at the plate. Therefore, players must become aware of what they are saying to themselves, and even more important, they must determine whether their self-statements are positive or negative.

In order to change negative self-talk, or *pressure* thoughts, into positive self-talk, or *action* thoughts, a player must first be aware of her self-talk patterns. Keeping a journal and logging self-talk can help players become aware of thoughts that support or undermine performance. Players should start a journal by responding to questions such as the following:

1. What do I say to myself before competition?
2. What do I say to myself when I am hitting?
3. What do I say to myself when I transition from offense to defense and defense to offense?

4. What thoughts accompany my best performances?
5. What thoughts accompany my poor performances?
6. Are most of my comments about my teammates, the coaches, the situation, or myself?

Figure 1.7 will help players discover ways to build their confidence by changing self-talk patterns.

Figure 1.7   Changing Self-Talk Patterns

Instructions: Confident players consistently display more positive self-beliefs than players who are less confident. These beliefs are messages that players say to themselves during the course of practice and competition. Players have the capacity to control their self-talk by converting "pressure" thoughts to "action" thoughts. The following are some examples.

Situation	Pressure Thought	Action Thought
You are playing a tough team.	We might not have the stuff to beat this team.	I'll follow the team plan and play my best.
You're on deck before an important at-bat.	I just have to get a hit.	Be patient and wait for a good pitch.
Your team is behind in a game.	I hope I don't strike out.	I'll do what I can to get on base.
You just swung at a bad pitch.	How could I be so stupid?	Refocus—this at-bat isn't over yet.
Pitcher is off to a bad start.	Way to put us in a hole early.	It's still early; work it one pitch at a time.
You've just made a throwing error.	I've let the whole team down.	Bring it on; I'll get it on the next play.

Personal Affirmations

Another way for a player to generate positive self-beliefs is by using personal affirmations or positive self-statements that direct her attention to her capabilities and potential. These statements inspire and motivate a player by helping her focus on what she wants to do and what she can do, rather than on what she cannot do. Players should create their own personal affirmations. They should write them down and repeat them often, particularly when they begin to think negatively or need a boost of inspiration. Here are some sample affirmations:

I love softball.

I can do this.

I feel strong.

I will try my hardest in practice today.

I am willing to give all I have for this team.

When the pressure is on, I come through.

I feel confident.

I know I'm going to get a hit.

The ball has no chance when I am at bat.

I feel ready for this game.

Although players can use various strategies to increase confidence, the role that coaches play in influencing player confidence should not be underestimated. How coaches interact with their players is one of the most important predictors of player confidence. If a coach expresses even the slightest bit of doubt about individual or team ability, confidence will suffer and so too will performance. Coaches must genuinely believe in every player and must convey this belief. Through personal interactions, instruction, and feedback, coaches directly and indirectly communicate their perceptions of player ability on a daily basis. Recent sport science research suggests that a coach's perception of athlete confidence is directly related to actual athlete performance. And confident athletes are successful athletes. Therefore, it is certainly worth every coach's while to build a player's confidence.

MENTAL IMAGERY

Mental imagery refers to the ability to create experiences in the mind. People use mental imagery on a daily basis, both consciously and unconsciously. It is one of the most commonly practiced psychological skills among North American Olympic athletes. There are two theories about how mental imagery works. Sport researchers believe that practicing vivid images causes the nerves that innervate certain muscle groups to transmit low-level impulses, which mimic the actual muscular contractions that occur during physical performance. Others contend that imagery aids performance by simply allowing athletes to mentally rehearse sport skills, thus reinforcing the physical demands of athletic tasks.

Regardless of the reason, using mental imagery as a form of skills training has shown to improve performance among many athletes. Performance is enhanced when players use imagery as a method for practicing physical and psychological skills. In order for mental imagery to affect performance, the images must be vivid and controllable. According to sport psychologist Terry Orlick, "[The] ultimate objective is to experience an ideal performance with all your senses." For players to use mental imagery most effectively, they should engage all five senses as they create mental images of performance situations:

Auditory: Hear what is taking place (cheering, ball hitting bat)

Olfactory: Smell the scents present (freshly cut grass, glove leather)

Taste: Note the tastes experienced (salty sweat, cool water)

Touch/kinesthetics: Feel the actions taking place (bat in hands, caught ball)

Visual: See the situation (fielding a ball, stepping into batter's box)

Players can use the sample scripts that follow to practice and test their mental imagery skills.

Mental Imagery Script #1

Instructions: To practice your ability to use mental imagery, read the following script and imagine the situation described. Then specify how well you were able to create the images in your mind.

Imagine a new softball . . . bright yellow . . . notice the seams and stitches . . . see the color of the stitches . . . bright red . . . notice the roundness of the ball . . . feel the leather as you grip the ball . . . feel the roughness of the seams on your fingertips as you rotate the ball in your hand . . . squeeze the ball . . . feeling the firmness.

Imagine receiving the ball in your glove. You immediately reach for the ball with your throwing hand to prepare for a throw . . . you rotate the ball in your hand, moving your fingers across the seams until you find the perfect grip . . . while rotating the ball, your arm

(continued)

(continue)

is coming around to the throwing position . . . your eyes are fixed on your target. Feel yourself throwing the ball . . . notice the seams rolling off the end of your fingertips as you release the ball . . . you hear the crisp sound of the ball hitting the glove. The ball is now old and worn . . . notice the scuffs and nicks . . . the bright yellow is now a dull color . . . it is the color of softball.

Rating: Specify how well you were able to use visual, auditory, and kinesthetic senses.

While reading the script, I was able to do the following (check all that apply):

____ See the ball

____ See the color

____ See the stitches

____ See the roundness

____ Feel the firmness of the ball

____ Feel the movement when throwing the ball

____ Hear the crisp sound of ball hitting glove

Mental Imagery Script #2

Instructions: To test your ability to use mental imagery, read the following script and imagine the situation described. Then specify how well you were able to create the images in your mind.

Imagine that you are standing in your primary position . . . notice the view to your left . . . what do you see? . . . who is in that direction? . . . what is to your right? . . . imagine glancing over your right shoulder . . . what do you see? . . . what is at your feet? . . . look down . . . is it freshly cut grass or smooth infield dirt that was just dragged for the game? You look up and notice a runner on first base . . . a left-handed slapper is coming to the plate . . . see yourself adjusting to the situation . . . you see the pitch and notice that the slapper lays down a bunt . . . the runner is advancing to second . . . what do you do? Imagine responding to the play . . . the play is over . . . you look ahead to prepare for the next batter . . . what do you see when you look straight ahead? . . . where are you focused?

Rating: Specify how well you were able to use the sense of vision and kinesthetics.

While reading the script, I was able to do the following (check all that apply):

_____ See the field

_____ See what would be to my left

_____ See what would be to my right

_____ See the grass or dirt

_____ See the batter

_____ See the bunt

_____ See and feel the completion of the play

Mental Imagery Problems

Unlike energy regulation, concentration, and confidence, problems with mental imagery do not have a direct negative impact on performance. Mental imagery is more of a performance enhancer than a performance necessity. Problems associated with the use of mental imagery are usually related to a player's inability to create vivid and controllable images. If a player cannot enrich the image with all of the relevant senses, vividness is minimized. In order for a player to "see" her performance as she would like to perform, the image must be as realistic as possible—hence the importance of engaging all five senses. A second concern is when players are unable to control their images. Some players can generate images of themselves in action, but their performances in these images are riddled with errors. When this is the case, mental imagery will not benefit performance. Players must be able to control a mental image and create a close-to-perfect picture of the desired action.

Improving Mental Imagery

Several strategies can be used to learn and enhance mental imagery skills. Beginning imagery training is most effective when players are relaxed. The imagery drills in this book focus on teaching players to create vivid images and to control those images. The drills include internal imagery (the player sees the image as if she is performing) and external imagery (the player sees the image as if she is seeing herself on videotape). Both of these vantage points are effective for mental training. The primary mental imaging technique used in the drills is performance imagery—the mental rehearsal of specific softball skills. The drills also enable players to practice using pre-performance routines. These routines are a good way to implement the use of mental imagery during competition.

The goal of this book is to provide softball players and coaches with concrete strategies to practice mental skills in conjunction with physical skills. The information presented in this chapter can be used to help ensure that practice time is spent training the whole player: body and mind.

Thinking the Game

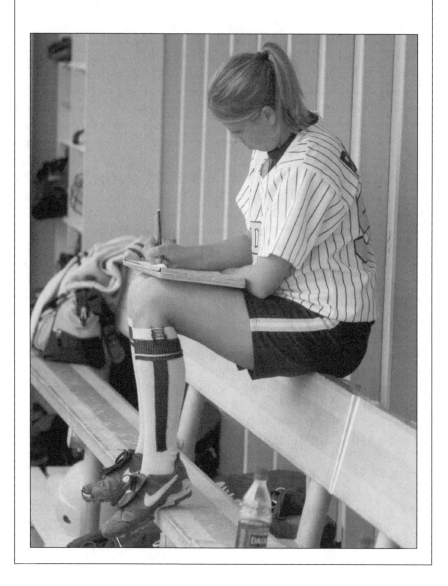

In many ways, the game of softball is comparable to the game of chess. In softball, each player is responsible for carrying out a distinct role that is often designated by her position. Similarly, in chess, each piece contributes to the game by performing a specific function. Playing the game of chess requires learning how each piece can move, but truly understanding the game requires learning the strategy behind each movement. If a beginning player is always told what piece to move and where to move it, this player will not develop an understanding of the fundamental processes of the game. To truly understand the game of chess, the player must know *why* the move is important.

The same theory applies to the game of softball. If a coach tells a player where to throw the ball and when to throw it, without also teaching the strategy behind those actions, the player will never truly understand the game. During the course of a game, crucial decisions must be made in very short time frames—sometimes in a split second. Softball players encounter complex situations with little time to make the most effective response. One of the quickest decisions a player must make is determining whether or not to swing at a pitch. When a pitch is delivered, the hitter has only milliseconds to recognize the pitch, determine the location of the pitch, and decide whether or not she is going to swing the bat. After she makes her decision, she must then give herself the command to put her body in motion or hold back. The amount of time that the player has to think is very minimal, so she must be mentally prepared before the pitch is thrown. She can examine her options and prepare herself by noting the pitcher's tendencies, determining what the situation calls for, and choosing the general location of the pitch she would like to hit. If a coach tells players when to swing, but does not explain the reasons why they should or should not swing at a specific pitch, the players will have difficulty making these kinds of quick decisions on their own.

Although it may not be as important for the novice or intermediate level player, thinking the game is a necessity as players climb the competitive ladder. As the competitive level increases, the role of each player becomes more demanding, and coaches can no longer take responsibility for the actions of every player on the team. To maximize team performance, each player should be able to think and respond to any situation that may arise on the playing field. If coaches are doing their job right, players will be able to take responsibility for thinking and acting on their own.

Although the physical aspects of sport are the most visible, it is the mental decisions and reactions that form the true foundation of solid athletic performance. Olympic softball players have said that achieving performance excellence is 70 to 80 percent mental. As the level of competition increases, so too does the significance of the mental game. When reflecting on your childhood sport experience, you may remember how easy the game seemed. Your performance then was probably 90 percent physical. You never worried about the outcome. You never had to think. You just played. You just reacted to the situation. That was when playing was easy. At the elite level, it is just the opposite. The game is no longer a physical battle, but a mental battle. At the elite level, all athletes have the requisite physical skills to perform well (or they wouldn't have reached that level). But when the talent level of two athletes is equal, the athlete with the stronger mind is the one who will prevail. Most athletic contests are won by the team with the most confidence, emotional control, and resilience.

The sport of softball has a significant amount of downtime. Unlike sports such as soccer, hockey, and basketball, softball action occurs in spurts of only a few seconds. In fact, research on baseball games found that in a three-hour game, the actual time spent in activity was just over four minutes. Similarly, a game of softball has a low percentage of time in action. So not only must softball players make quick decisions, whether batting or fielding, but they must also deal with the inactivity that is part of the game. Although this time gives a player the opportunity to plan for the next play or situation, it sometimes allows too much time to think. These thoughts can have a positive or negative influence on player performance. Therefore, players must learn to "think the game" from a variety of angles.

THE MIND GAME

When people think about what it takes to be a successful athlete at the elite level, certain qualities usually come to mind. These qualities will include both physical and mental components. Although coaches discuss the importance of mental toughness, they still tend to focus on physical skills because these skills are observable and easy to judge. Mental skills, on the other hand, do not receive much attention because they are intangible and much more difficult to assess. Coaches can refer to figure 2.1 to generate

Figure 2.1 Qualities of Elite Athletes

To initiate a team discussion, ask your players to identify the qualities that elite athletes possess. Tell your players to think of Olympic athletes such as Dot Richardson or Lisa Fernandez. How did these players become so great? What characteristics make up their personality? What makes them so successful? Create a separate list of physical and mental characteristics as in the following example. (You will probably notice that the mental characteristics outnumber the physical by a substantial amount.)

Physical	Mental
Strong	Confident
Quick	Motivated
Fit	Focused

After compiling the list of qualities, lead a discussion about the importance of each mental quality. Then discuss what it means to possess each quality; ask questions pertaining to what it feels like and what it looks like to exhibit each of the qualities. For example, most players will list confidence as a necessary attribute for athletic success, but rarely will they have thought about what confidence truly means. So if your players list this as an important quality, you might first define confidence. Then ask questions such as, "What does it mean to have confidence?" "What does having confidence feel like?" "What does it look like?" and "What can we do to increase our confidence as a team?" To make it fun, have some players get up and demonstrate what it looks like. Not only will this help your players understand the importance of each mental characteristic, but it will also give them an idea about how to think and act as a team. You may also want to use this activity to develop your expectations for player behavior on and off the field.

a discussion with their team about the importance of mental skills for superior athletic performance.

COMPETITIVENESS

Competitiveness is a state of mind that leads the body to action. It is an attitude that encompasses passion, grit, mental toughness, and the utmost desire to win. A competitive player is one who is intense, takes risks, and plays with authority. She is the kind of player who wants to be at the plate when the game is on the line, wants to get the job done, and consistently comes through in the clutch.

Competitiveness is a mandatory quality for athletic success. It is also a quality that can be developed and improved. Becoming a competitive player requires a commitment to mental preparation and readiness. To play competitively in games, players must also play competitively in practice. A hard working, persistent player in practice is more likely to bring that work ethic onto the field during competition. Coaches who conduct effective practices will reduce the mental mistakes that their players make during competition. Using a mentaphysical approach in practice enables coaches to develop great competitors who are capable of achieving performance excellence.

PRINCIPLES OF PERFORMANCE EXCELLENCE

Performing well doesn't happen by accident or chance. Players spend years training in an attempt to achieve performance excellence. Performance excellence means a player performs the best she can given the physical (e.g., flexibility), psychological (e.g., anxiety), and situational (e.g., away game) constraints. The fewer or more manageable the constraints, the closer the player is to achieving performance excellence. Coaches should use a mentaphysical approach to help players develop a competitive attitude that allows them to overcome these constraints. There are five psychological states associated with performance excellence in softball: a passion to play, willingness to sacrifice the self, trust in ability, knowledge of the process, and resilience to overcome mistakes and failures. Coaches should encourage their players to adopt these five *principles of performance excellence.*

Passion

Passion for the sport is a prerequisite to pursuing performance excellence. Passion causes a player to have motivation, dedication, persistence, and a strong overall work ethic on and off the field. A player with passion for the game is a player who can't wait to practice, puts everything on the line, and gives 100 percent regardless of the score or circumstance. Coaches, teammates, and fans may describe this player as one who "plays the game with heart." A passionate player fights to the end even when she knows that her opponent has already won.

Self-Sacrifice

Sacrifice is more than just showing up to practice each day; it is what a player is willing to do both on and off the softball field for the good of her team. Sacrificing the self is when a player totally and completely dedicates herself to her team and her sport with utmost integrity and respect. Sacrifice comes in different forms. On the field, a player may sacrifice herself by laying down a bunt to advance one of her teammates or sacrificing her body to make an extraordinary defensive play. Off the field, a player may sacrifice some of her socializing time to make sure that she is completely ready when it is time to play. This may include getting enough sleep, eating well, staying fit, and finishing homework (not only to ensure that she is eligible to play, but also to dedicate herself to being the best she can be).

Some players view their sport as a duty and complain about what they must do or what they aren't allowed to do. They complain about practice, teammates, and coach decisions. Obviously, this kind of attitude can be detrimental to team performance. If a player truly wants to achieve her highest potential in a team setting, she must be willing to listen, compromise, and do anything she can to support a common goal. Ultimately, the opportunity to play the sport of softball should be appreciated because it is not a duty, but a privilege. A player who embodies the idea of true sacrifice will think about how her decisions affect others and not just about how they affect herself.

Trust

A player must trust in her ability, and in the ability of her coaches and teammates, to perform under any circumstance. A player may be gifted with natural athletic ability, but if she questions this ability, her performance will decline. When a player does not trust in her natural ability, she will begin to force her actions instead of just reacting to the situation. For example, a talented shortstop who repeatedly overthrows first base may be aiming the ball instead of just letting it go. Although an overthrow may seem like a physical error, it is more likely the result of a mental lapse caused by worry or by the thought of making an error. In addition, a lack of trust may cause a player to hesitate and question a decision such as where to throw the ball or whether she should make a throw. A player who trusts in her ability will not have to think in this type of situation; instead, she will allow her body to react because she knows that it will automatically make the correct physical response. This trust allows a player to acknowledge that sound training has created a well-oiled machine that can be given the freedom to perform on "automatic pilot." When a player can control her mind, and she knows when to think and when to simply react, this allows the body to perform physically without mental static interfering with the action.

A player must not only trust in her own abilities, but also the abilities of her teammates because the completion of a play in softball is typically dependent upon two or more players. Another situation that may cause a player to hesitate is when she must throw the ball to a teammate whom she does not trust. Maybe she doesn't think the player is good enough, or maybe she doesn't think her teammate will get to the base in time to receive her throw. In either case, even the slightest bit of doubt will lead to a breakdown in team performance. Instead of questioning or getting frustrated, players should lead their teammates in the right direction and let them know their expectations of each other. A player should emphasize what she wants her teammates to do instead of what she thinks they cannot do or are not doing.

Defensive players do not have time to doubt. An automatic reaction is required in order to get the out.

Trusting in the coach is a necessity for team success for several reasons. Coaches are the ones who make the lineup, call the plays, and teach the players how to perform. If a team does not trust in their coach's decisions, they will be reluctant to execute his or her wishes. Some players may even become outwardly defiant, and this will hurt overall team chemistry. To get players to buy into a coach's system, the coach should convince them that each and every decision is made for the good of the team.

Knowledge

Players must give priority to the process and not just the outcome. This involves focusing on the present—on their performance of the current action—instead of focusing on the results of those actions. In softball, it is common to see a player who consistently hits the ball well during practice but never makes solid contact during games. In practice, many hitting drills involve a pitching machine or a hitting tee, neither of which truly imitate what it is like to hit off of a live pitcher. These types of drills offer a very controlled environment. Therefore, it is fairly easy for players to perform well because they do not have to guess about the type of pitch or where it will be thrown. Because they are hitting the ball well in these conditions, many hitters are more concerned with how hard they hit and where the ball goes versus how well they perform their swing. Unfortunately, hitting well in practice does not always carry over into games, especially if players are not using correct technique.

In addition to using their knowledge of the process when performing a physical skill, players should also focus on the processes behind game strategies, performing under pressure, bouncing back after failure, and overall mental toughness. If a player is able to stay in the present and focus on the process of each action, she will be more likely to achieve the desired outcome.

Resilience

All players make mistakes. This is the norm in sport and not the exception. Therefore, players must be able to overcome their mistakes and be resilient in the face of failure or disappointment. Resilience involves the ability to let go of errors and return to the present. A resilient player learns from each mistake and uses it as an opportunity to improve. Athletes put a lot of pressure on themselves to perform, but they should always keep in mind that success doesn't depend on one at-bat or one fielding play. Although it would be nice if players could be perfect in every situation, especially those situations that may determine the outcome of a game, this is just not realistic. But when players do not perform well in these situations, they often forget that it is not that one at-bat or that one play that caused the loss. There are usually multiple chances for more than one team member to score that decisive run or make a critical play throughout the course of a game. So a player must remember that she will get another chance to do it right; there will be many more opportunities to get the big hit or make the big play. She must learn from the situation, make an adjustment, and be prepared to achieve success in the future. If a player is not resilient, she will continually struggle and question her ability to be a consistent player.

Players can use a four-step process to learn how to be resilient and overcome fielding and hitting errors. The frustration players feel after making a mistake can be detrimental to future efforts, so this method helps players channel their frustration into constructive energy. After an error, a player should mentally go through these four steps: One, the player *Acknowledges* that she made a mistake and is frustrated. Two, she *Reviews* the situation by asking herself, "What happened to create this outcome?" Three, she *Strategizes* to determine what she would do differently if the situation were to arise again. Four, she *Executes* by preparing herself for the next play. Players can use this process to get their *ARSE* in gear after making errors. Although it is a simple strategy, it will not work for all players. Some players lack resiliency and cannot get their mind off of the errors. When a player cannot shift her attention back to the game, her mind will be consumed with negative thoughts about the bad play, and she will not focus on the current game situation. Subsequently, another error is likely to follow. These players often lose momentum, choke, and do not play up to their potential.

The five principles of performance excellence can be learned and can enhance player performance if coaches truly make a commitment to the mentaphysical approach to training. Another way to enhance mental skills is through the development of routines.

ROUTINE DEVELOPMENT

Routines are a part of everyday life. Many people have a routine from the time they wake up in the morning to the time they go to bed at night. If you think about it, you have probably standardized the sequence of your daily habits, such as your bathing routine. You no longer have to think about the order in which you wash your face, brush your teeth, and comb your hair; you do it automatically in the same sequence each day. By the time your morning routine is complete, you are ready for the day. Similarly, in sport settings, athletes and coaches commonly develop routines with the belief that they will assist performance.

The primary way that routines benefit performance is by promoting consistency. If a player continues to do something the same way, she can expect to receive the same results. Therefore, if she achieves the desired results, she should prepare in the same manner, but if she does not achieve the desired results, she should make a change. Players need to know how to mentally and physically prepare in order to achieve the most desirable results. Once a player determines the combination of behaviors that helps prepare her to play her best, she should perform these activities in the same sequence each time so that her actions become automated. For example, players should develop a sequence of thoughts and behaviors to perform before stepping into the batter's box for every at-bat. This will allow a player to automate her preparation so that she primes herself in the same manner each time, which will lead to more consistent results.

In the sport of softball, there are two types of routines: pre-competition and pre-performance routines. Pre-competition routines involve a sequence of behaviors that mentally and physically prepare a player for optimal performance before a game. Pre-performance routines are a sequence of behaviors that prepare a player for the execution of a single skill.

Pre-competition Routines

Preparation for competition should not begin immediately before a game. For optimal performance, pre-game preparation should begin at least one day before a game or tournament. Before competition, players need to have a clear mind to facilitate game readiness. The key components to a pre-competition routine should include the following:

- **Planning.** Because a softball coach must attend to the needs of 20 to 25 players with distinct personalities, pre-competition planning can be a challenge. The pre-game routine for an introverted, shy player may be quite different than for an outgoing extrovert. One player may prefer to spend time alone or in quiet interaction with a few teammates before playing, while another player may choose a more stimulating setting with raucous team interactions. Therefore, to help players shape their pre-game routines, coaches must know each player as an individual.

- **Rest.** The night before a game, players should make sure that they get an ample amount of sleep. Some players will need more sleep than others, but each player should know how much sleep she needs to perform her best. Players must also know how long it takes for them to be fully alert after waking up. If it takes two hours for a player to be completely alert in the morning, it is not a good idea for her to wake up one hour before she is due at the field on game day. This also applies if the game is later in the day and the player decides to take an afternoon nap.

When teams are playing in tournaments, resting between games is also important, not only to allow players to relax their bodies, but also to allow them to relax their minds. A player should gauge the amount of rest depending on how much time there is between games. If she has a lot of time, a nap could be beneficial. If time is limited, she might just want to take a short time-out to rest her eyes, or take her mind off of the game by socializing with others. The need for rest depends on the individual. Therefore, players should pay attention to their resting patterns and use that information to achieve an optimal state for performance.

Players should also be aware of the amount of energy they expend the day before a game. Team practice on the day before competition should be more mental than physical. To conserve energy, players should limit the number of repetitions and spend time mentally preparing for the next day's opponent. Therefore, the emphasis in practice is on the quality versus the quantity of physical tasks. This may include analyzing game strategies, reviewing opponent statistics, and using mental imagery to prepare for competition.

- **Nutrition.** The night before competition, players should eat a well-balanced meal that is not too light or too heavy. They need to make sure it provides enough fuel for the day of the game. Pasta dishes are often a good meal choice the night before a game. On game day, players should have a nutritious breakfast. This is one of the most important meals of the day because it is what nourishes the body after a long night's rest. A player's breakfast should be something that is substantial enough to give her energy, but not too heavy. A big breakfast may sit in her stomach and weigh her down during competition. Throughout the day, it is important for players to keep their body replenished. They should be constantly drinking water to keep the body hydrated. Little snacks, such as fruit or energy bars, can also fulfill energy needs. Similar to rest, eating patterns should be based on individual preferences.

• **Attitude.** Attitude is one of the few things in life a person has the ability to control. A pre-competition routine gives a player the opportunity to prepare for a game by adjusting her mind-set and getting herself into playing mode. A player should use this time to adopt an optimistic, positive, and competitive attitude that reinforces self-confidence. A team's attitude is largely dependent on the attitude of the coach. If a coach wants her players to be energetic and competitive, she must model these qualities and convey this message to her team. The coach should tell the players what attitude she expects them to adopt, how she wants them to think, and how she wants them to behave; she should also show the players what it looks like to have this attitude. Coaches must establish the characteristics that will represent the attitude of their team. (Refer back to figure 2.1 to determine various components of attitude.) A coach should remind players to take personal responsibility for their own attitude without worrying about others. If each player adopts the team attitude endorsed by the coach, the potential for team chemistry and overall team success will dramatically increase. It is the coach's responsibility to teach players when and how to "adjust their attitudes" in preparation for competition and it is the player's responsibility to make the adjustment.

• **Composure.** Composure is another central ingredient for game readiness; it is the behavioral component of attitude. After developing the attitude that the team will adopt, a coach can use the qualities that represent that attitude to explain the idea of composure. Developing a certain type of demeanor begins in practice. Staying composed during a game means staying in control—in control of emotions, in control of decisions, and in control of physical efforts. To stay in control, a player must be able to properly regulate her energy. If a player gets overly excited, she will no longer have complete control over her actions. Another aspect of composure for any team is confidence. As mentioned earlier, it is easy to see whether or not a player is confident. Maintaining composure means that a player will exhibit a confident demeanor regardless of the situation. Through the use of the mentaphysical drills, coaches can directly address the mental skills needed to maintain composure.

Team composure may also include how the players approach competition: how they warm up, how they wear their uniform, how they enter the facility, how they communicate on the field. There is some truth in the saying, "If you look sharp, you are more likely to play sharp." How a team looks has the potential to influence the opponent. If all team members wear their uniform the same, act confidently, play aggressively, and work well together during warm-ups, the opposing team will take notice. Developing the right demeanor and maintaining composure will only enhance the team's ability to gain a competitive edge over the opponent.

• **Mental rehearsal.** As game time approaches, players should consider conducting a mental rehearsal of the upcoming game as part of their pre-competition routine. This allows the player to prepare for a specific opponent by using mental imagery to practice and plan for competition. The mental rehearsal should precede the actual warm-up immediately before the game. Using positive self-talk and checking energy level are two additional mental strategies to employ just before the game (these can be used during stretching and warm-up drills). By using a pre-competition mental routine, a player can increase the likelihood that she will be able to compete at her highest level every time she steps on the field. See figure 2.2 for a worksheet to create a pre-competition routine.

Pre-performance Routines

Unlike sports that have continuous play (e.g., soccer), softball is a game of stops and starts. Before the initiation of each play, a softball player has the time and opportunity to conduct a pre-performance routine. These types of routines are particularly important to standardize performance. If a hitter wants to be focused and prepared for each and every pitch, she must begin her preparation the same way each time. Whether on offense or defense, players can benefit from pre-performance routines. Figure 2.3 contains a worksheet that can be used to create individualized pre-performance routines for various skills.

Figure 2.2   Pre-competition Routine Worksheet

Pre-competition routines should begin at least one day before a game or tournament. Maintaining a consistent sequence of behaviors to prepare for each game will ensure that the mind and body are fully prepared to perform at the most optimal level for success. Components of your pre-competition routine should include activities that will allow you to operate with a clear mind, at an optimal level of energy, and with confidence that you are prepared to play your best. Consider the activities in which you engage the night before competition to the start of the game such as sleep patterns, nutritional habits, homework, mental training exercises, and equipment preparation.

Night Before Competition

5:00 – 6:00pm	Arrive home from practice and take a shower
6:00 – 7:00pm	Eat dinner and debrief about the day with roommate
7:00 – 8:00pm	Work on homework
8:00 – 9:00pm	Finish homework and watch TV
9:00 – 10:00pm	Get uniform and equipment ready and rehearse positive affirmations
10:00 – 11:00pm	Do 10 minutes of mental imagery and go to bed

Morning of Competition

7:00 – 8:00am	Wake up and take a shower
8:00 – 9:00am	Eat breakfast, read the paper, and finish getting ready for the day
9:00 – 10:00am	Perform 10 minutes of mental imagery, pack up, and leave for the game
10:00 – 11:00am	Mentally prepare in the car, listen to music, focus attention, adjust attitude
11:00 – 12:00pm	Greet teammates, get warmed up, and scope the playing field
Game Time	Take the field with a confident, composed, and competitive attitude

Figure 2.3   Pre-performance Routine Worksheet

Pre-performance routines are important in developing performance consistency. Using an individualized pre-performance routine will allow you to prepare in a consistent manner to ensure a more consistent performance. There are three phases in a pre-performance routine: Prepare, Automate, Execute. To create your pre-performance routine, list the sequence of your thoughts and behaviors for each phase. You can use this worksheet to create an individualized pre-performance routine for any skill. See drill chapters for sample pre-performance routines.

Phase I: Prepare

Elements of preparation during phase I may include reviewing the previous situation, analyzing the current situation, and receiving information from the coach.

Phase I: Prepare

Phase II: Automate

After reviewing the situation in the *preparation* phase, players will now redirect their attention to the demands of the immediate task. This may include a sequence of specific thoughts and behaviors such as strategically planning for the play, thinking confidently, and performing a set of physical behaviors that the player rehearses in an identical manner each time she prepares for this situation, whether it be hitting, pitching, or fielding.

Phase II: Automate

Phase III: Execute

During the *execution* phase, players are in their ready position to perform, are focused on the ball, and will rehearse a self-talk statement to reinforce the desired outcome.

Phase III: Execute

Gayle Blevins has served as head softball coach at the University of Iowa for 17 seasons. In her entire career, she has won over 900 games, including four College World Series and eight Big Ten titles. She is in the National Fastpitch Coaches Association Hall of Fame and has earned both Big Ten and National Coach of the Year awards. She offers her favorite team drill which can be used to build confidence and practice pre-performance routines.

Photo courtesy of Gayle Blevins

Gayle Blevins, head coach, University of Iowa

Shadow

Mental Skill   To build confidence through pre-performance routines

Physical Skill   To quickly review all defensive and pitching responsibilities

Purpose   To review the defensive responsibilities while entire team rehearses varied situations and utilizes pre-performance routines

Implementation   All plays are made without a ball or a throw. Put all defensive players on the field at the same time (if you have several at one position, stack them up to rotate onto the field). In the next three to five minutes, instruct each player to go through all defensive aspects of their position, such as

- fielding imaginary ground balls, line drives, and fly balls
- practicing imaginary exchanges at bases (footwork for infielders, outfielders working on throws to bases), backups, cutoffs, and relays, and
- practicing communication with teammates.

Also, have players work on pre-performance and recovery routine. Force them to think in terms of a missed play, followed by recovery prior to the next pitch being delivered by the pitcher.

Coaching Tips

- Listen for proper pre-pitch conversation from your defensive players. If they fail to pre-plan, explain the importance of pre-performance conversation.
- Each player should work independently of the other defensive players; however, ask them to talk as if they are working together.

GAME READINESS

The concept of mental toughness refers to the optimal mind-set for competition. Players who are mentally tough thrive on the pressure associated with playing competitive softball. To prepare for these pressure situations, a player must practice under stress. Many of the mentaphysical drills are designed to mimic pressure situations and to allow players to master these conditions. For example, if a runner is on second base and a line drive is hit to the outfield, the fielder must quickly field the ball and make a throw on the runner who is advancing toward home plate. In this type of situation, the outfielder may get overly excited and rush her actions, or she may begin to worry about what her coaches and teammates will think if she doesn't make the play. Instead of waiting until game day to experience this type of situation, a player should experience it in practice when the environment is nonthreatening and she can take the risk without the fear of making a mistake. By encountering these situations in practice, players will be more ready and more comfortable coping with pressure when it arises during games.

Being prepared for pressure situations—in other words, being mentally tough—requires a player to adopt many of the attitudes and behaviors previously mentioned in this chapter. An enormous contributor to mental toughness is positive self-beliefs. Sustaining positive beliefs in the face of errors as well as successes will help a player maintain a winning attitude throughout the game. This increases the chances that she will give 100 percent effort for seven innings (or more if necessary). When encountering errors or mistakes, a player must focus on what she can control and rid her mind of what she cannot control. For example, when a batter strikes out looking, she may return to the dugout frustrated and upset over the umpire's call. She may express this frustration through negative behaviors such as throwing equipment or ignoring teammate support. Although she may believe this shows that she really cares, the actual result of this behavior is a negative impact on the attitude of her teammates. If she chooses to focus on the outcome of this situation, which is uncontrollable, it will be detrimental to her and the team's future performance. See figure 2.4 for an exercise designed to help softball players assess the controllable and uncontrollable aspects of competition.

To be adequately prepared, a player must enter the game knowing what can be controlled and what is outside of her immediate control. This will allow her to focus her attention and energy on factors that she has the power to change, thereby emphasizing the process and not the outcome. Directing attention to what a player can control, coupled with a competitive mind-set during the game, will help players enjoy the journey as well as the destination. Players need to remember that softball is a game. Satisfaction is not solely determined by wins and losses but rather by the feeling players get when they know that they were ready to compete and played the game well.

TRANSITIONS AND DOWNTIME

As previously mentioned, softball invites the opportunity to have too much time to think. Much of the actual time on the field is not spent performing. This downtime allows the players to expend mental energy on uncontrollable obstacles such as weather conditions and fatigue. In addition, when transitioning from offense to defense, and defense to offense, players are faced with unique mental challenges to sustain performance consistency. If there is a long offensive inning, a player might come out of the dugout feeling flat and lacking energy as she makes the transition to defense. A player must know her distinct roles and responsibilities, both offensively and defensively, so that she can direct her attention to the demands of each role. The mentaphysical drills in this book offer players concrete mental strategies for dealing with these situations. By using these drills, players will have the ability to rise to the challenge of playing a sport that consists of short, quick bursts of activity over a long period of time.

The time immediately following a game provides a great opportunity for the coach to address the team while the competition is

Figure 2.4   Control Factors

This exercise will help players think about how they use their mental energy. In the following illustration, the items listed in the "strike zone" are examples of issues that are within a player's immediate control. The items listed outside the strike zone are examples of issues that are not within a player's control. Each player should customize this worksheet based on her softball experience. She can add or omit items both within and outside of the strike zone. She should then estimate what percentage of her mental energy is spent on issues inside and outside of her control. The goal is to help the player realize how she uses her mental energy so she can begin focusing most of that energy on issues that she can control.

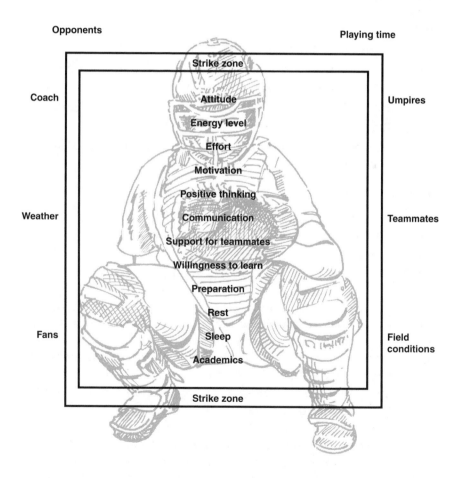

Opponents

Playing time

Coach

Umpires

Weather

Teammates

Fans

Field conditions

Strike zone

Attitude

Energy level

Effort

Motivation

Positive thinking

Communication

Support for teammates

Willingness to learn

Preparation

Rest

Sleep

Academics

Strike zone

still fresh in everyone's mind. This is a good time to evaluate goals. What were the team goals for that game? Did the team meet some of their goals? Which goals did they not meet? What obstacles confronted the team? What will they do differently next time? Players typically know what they did or didn't do well during the course of a game. Instead of telling them about what they did wrong, the coach should try to focus on what they did right and what they could do better next time. An open conversation with the team allows learning, goal evaluation, and problem solving to take place. This will help prepare the players for future games. Here are some suggestions on topics to address and avoid during post-game discussions:

Dos

- Acknowledge good teamwork
- Allow players to bring up their own mistakes and tell them how each mistake can be corrected
- Emphasize goals that were met and emphasize team mission
- Reinforce the contributions of all players, including those who did not compete

Don'ts

- Don't emphasize one player over another
- Don't harangue players who make mistakes
- Don't overemphasize unmet goals
- Don't tell the team they are not good enough

Most coaches have mastered the physical components of softball; many are savvy about the tactics of smart play; but few are able to fully develop the mental qualities in their players that will help them excel. The purpose of the following seven chapters is to offer the serious coach and player the resources to learn how to "think the game" before, during, and after competition. The emphasis is on the premise of the mentaphysical approach—players will learn how to use mental skills effectively if those skills are taught simultaneously with physical skills. Figure 2.5 can be used to help coaches and players evaluate their performance for each drill that fits their position. A sample entry is listed to get started.

Figure 2.5 Drill Evaluation Form

Instructions: Each athlete will have her own drill evaluation form. Select relevant drills and record scores after each practice.

- Drill Name: Include drills from practice which have scoring components
- Player Scores: Record scores for each drill
- Evaluation: Record improvements for each drill
- Performance Notes: Record notes pertaining to mental and physical aspects of skill performance

Name: _____   Position: _____

Drill Name	Player Scores				Evaluation	Notes
	Week 1	Week 2	Week 3	Week 4		
Drill #1: Stayin' Alive					Continued to improve. Improvement score for the month is 7. Goal is to reach 20 hits in 3 more weeks.	Breathing exercise has been helpful. Need to relax hands and remember to pivot back foot.

3

Hitting

Hitting a softball is one of the most challenging sport skills. Some athletic skills, such as making a tackle in football, require a burst of speed or power that is generated by large fast-twitch muscle fibers. Other skills, such as shooting a free throw, require accuracy and very controlled movements that are maintained by slow-twitch muscle fibers. Unlike these types of skills, striking a softball requires a unique combination of both power (to swing the bat) and accuracy (to hit the ball). To make the skill even more difficult, a hitter must possess exceptional hand–eye coordination so that she can perfectly time her movements to make a solid connection between two moving objects. Along with being one of the most challenging sport skills, consistent and timely hitting provides the key ingredient that often makes the difference between winning and losing a ball game. If a team is able to consistently hit the ball, they are more likely to get on base; and if they are more likely to get on base, they are more likely to score runs; and if they are more likely to score runs, they are more likely to win games.

Many of the existing softball books address hitting as a science because the movements of the skill are so complex. To determine the most efficient hitting mechanics for speed, accuracy, and power, biomechanists have studied the skill of hitting in terms of levers, angles, torques, and forces. From the initial stance, hand placement, and bat position to the stride, pivot, and follow-through, each component of the swing has been broken down and explained in great detail. Using this information, many coaches develop their own philosophy about the proper mechanics of hitting and teach their players a specific style. Practice time is then devoted to repetitious drills that help players learn and develop each component of the hitting style. In turn, many players perform the skill very well with automated movements that require a minimal amount of effort or thought. But interestingly, some of the most successful hitters have the worst swings, and some of the worst hitters have the best swings. So one might ask, are the mechanics of hitting exclusively a physical science?

Although many coaches emphasize practicing and perfecting the physical components of hitting such as balance, hip rotation, and quick hands, becoming a successful hitter is much more complex than developing a swing that is mechanically sound. It requires anticipation, early pitch recognition, quick decision making, patience, and a timely response that involves swinging the bat on a plane that matches the path of the ball. This sequence of events becomes even more complex when a player is instructed to execute a play at a specific time or to hit the ball to a particular location for strategic purposes. Although coaches recognize the importance of using mental skills to successfully perform this sequence of events, these skills are rarely taught. Successful hitting is largely dependent on the player's ability to control and maintain an intricate balance between mind and body.

This chapter is not designed to teach the physical components of hitting. It is up to the coach to teach the players his or her own style of hitting. The drills in this chapter are intended to supplement a team's hitting philosophy by helping coaches and players integrate mental skills into physical practice to bring the team to a new level of performance. The drills are designed to accommodate all skill levels and can be easily adapted to meet various performance goals. It is never too early to start teaching and practicing both the mental and physical aspects of the game because these abilities will often carry over into daily life. Players will learn to control their mind and body in any situation on and off the field, producing well-rounded athletes, but more importantly, well-rounded individuals.

ENERGY REGULATION

What good are sound mechanics when it's the bottom of the seventh, with two outs, two runners on base, and the hitter, who just took strike two, is overcome by a surge of muscle tension when she realizes that she *has* to get a hit or her team will lose the game? During highly intense situations, even the most talented player can fail to execute a well-learned skill. For most players, pressure situations elicit an emotional response that is accompanied by a heightened level of arousal or excitement. A hitter may interpret these feelings as either positive or negative, and this interpretation will have an enormous impact on the outcome of that particular at-bat. A hitter who wants to be at the plate when the game is on the line demonstrates a positive interpretation of heightened arousal. This hitter seeks challenges, thrives under pressure, and rises to the occasion, matching her skills to the demands of the situation. Another hitter may perceive the situation as threatening, focus on the outcome rather than the task, be frightened by the thought of failure, and change her mind-set from "I'm going to get a hit" to "I have to get a hit." This is an example of a negative interpretation of heightened arousal. When this hitter's energy or arousal level exceeds a zone that is comfortable, she experiences performance anxiety, which may invoke various physiological changes such as sweaty palms, muscle tension, increased heart rate, and a narrowing of attention.

In the previous example, the player demonstrated a negative interpretation of arousal, which led to an increase in muscle tension. At this point, her coach might offer words of encouragement such as "You can do it" or "Just relax," but without practice it is very difficult in these situations to get the mind to regain control of the body. Unlike a hitter who may interpret the situation positively, this hitter will not rise to the occasion, but will most likely suffer the consequences of performance anxiety. She might feel confident, she might be determined to get a hit, and she might have the best hitting mechanics in the world, but when she swings the bat, her movements will be rigid and jerky. The bat will not flow smoothly on an even plane through the strike zone, and the hitter's chances of making solid contact with the ball will decline. Consequently, this sequence of events will most likely result in an outcome that is commonly known as "choking under pressure."

At some point, every hitter will be confronted with an emotional situation that elicits a change in arousal. Imagine that you are a player whose team is playing in a championship game against a team that is ranked number one in the nation. It's the bottom of the seventh inning, the score is tied, and you haven't played the entire game. All of a sudden, with two outs and a runner on third, your coach unexpectedly puts you in to pinch hit. You know that your performance at the plate could mean the difference between winning and losing. Your heart begins to race, you feel the adrenaline flowing throughout your body, and you want to get a hit so badly that you become anxious.

Although this example is extreme, a tremendous number of hitting situations elicit increases in energy. Maybe a hitter is trying to earn a spot in the starting lineup, experiencing her first at-bat of the season, or facing an old teammate who is now pitching for the opposing team. In fact, most situations will cause a hitter to feel excited or anxious when she steps into the batter's box. It is rare for a hitter to step into the box and feel sluggish or too tired to swing the bat. Even during a slump or when facing a pitcher who is throwing a no-hitter, just the thought of stepping into the batter's box is enough to get the competitive juices flowing. Therefore, the majority of hitting drills regarding arousal regulation will focus on strategies for decreasing energy.

Before a hitter practices regulating her energy, she must identify the energy level that will maximize her hitting ability. The amount of energy necessary for optimal performance depends on the needs of the individual and will vary from one hitter to another. Some batters will perform better at highly intense levels, while others will perform better when calm and relaxed. To help identify their optimal energy level, players should recall past successful at-bats. Players should then record their optimal energy level for hitting. Once an optimal level is identified, players can practice a variety of techniques to achieve and maintain this level when over or underaroused. With practice, players will become proficient at controlling and maintaining their energy at a level that will decrease performance anxiety and increase their chances of getting a hit. Refer to chapter 1 for energy assessment tools and for additional energy regulation strategies that may be integrated as variations into the drills.

Energy Under Pressure

The most common time for a hitter to experience changes in her energy is during a pressure situation. Sometimes pressure is created by the situation, and sometimes the player puts pressure on herself in an attempt to achieve a performance goal. Therefore, it is important to provide hitters with opportunities to respond to pressure situations during practice. If a hitter becomes proficient at using strategies to increase and decrease her energy in practice, she will be more likely to be able to control her energy and maintain an optimal level when performing in games. This will give her the best opportunity for successful at-bats. She will also be less likely to negatively interpret changes in energy, which often leads to performance anxiety. Drill 1: Stayin' Alive is designed to teach hitters a breathing strategy to regulate energy level.

In the on-deck circle, a hitter should assess the current game situation, including where the defense is positioned, how the defense responds to each pitch, the speed of the pitcher, the sequence of pitches being thrown, the runners on base, the number of outs, and so forth. This information gives the hitter an idea about what to expect when she approaches the plate. When it is her turn to bat, she knows what she wants to do and what pitch she should look for to accomplish her goal. Just before she steps into the batter's box, she will look down the third-base line to receive the signs from her coach. At this point, the coach may instruct the hitter to execute a specific play such as a hit-and-run or a bunt, which may cause the hitter to change her initial mind-set. The hitter may respond to this situation by putting extra pressure on herself, not only to execute the task, but also to please her coach. This can lead to a heightened level of arousal, making her vulnerable to performance anxiety. To avoid this outcome, drill 2: Pressure Ball can be used to help hitters learn to regulate their energy while adapting to various pressure situations.

Managing Muscle Tension

Muscle tension is one of the most frequent responses to changes in energy that occur during pressure situations. A variety of factors may contribute to an increased amount of tension in the batter's box. It could be the result of performance anxiety, frustration, or simply the high level of intensity at which many players compete. The ability to control muscle tension is especially important for hitting because hitting involves the coordination of many body segments and large muscle groups. If these muscles do not function together properly, performance will suffer. Following is a simple exercise that demonstrates the impact of muscle tension on motor performance.

Muscle Tension and Performance

To experience firsthand how muscle tension affects performance, you can perform a simple finger-tapping exercise using your index and middle fingers. First, tense these fingers and try tapping them back and forth very rapidly on a hard surface. Now, relax the fingers and try tapping them back and forth again. You will notice that when you allowed your muscles to relax, you were able to tap your fingers much faster. When your fingers were tense, the muscles that were functioning to move the fingers up were working against the muscles that were functioning to move the fingers down, making it difficult to move them in either direction. When your fingers were relaxed, the two sets of muscle groups worked together by tensing and relaxing in an alternating fashion. This allowed each set of muscles to perform its job smoothly without interference or resistance. Although players do not spend time tapping their fingers in the batter's box, this concept can be applied in the same manner when coordinating the movements of the larger muscle groups, such as the biceps and triceps, that are used to swing the bat.

The first step in controlling muscle tension is becoming aware of the amount of tension inherent in performing a skill. The amount of muscle tension necessary to perform a successful swing will vary for each player. Drill 3: Muscle Tension Awareness will help players determine their optimal level of muscle tension for hitting.

Most players can automatically perform the physical components of hitting without thinking about them. As a result, many players never consider or even notice the amount of muscle tension that is generated when swinging the bat. Unknowingly, many hitters have a natural tendency to grip the bat so tight that you would think somebody was trying to steal it. A hitter can learn to become more aware of her muscle tension by tensing and relaxing specific muscle groups before each swing. With practice, a player will become more familiar with her body and will be able to identify and regulate high and low levels of muscle tension without having to tense and relax her muscles. By gaining an awareness of variations in muscle tension, the player will be able to adequately control changes in tension that may occur during game situations. Drill 4: Mastering Your Muscle Tension will help players maximize muscular control while hitting. This drill teaches hitters to manage muscle tension by targeting problem areas.

1   Stayin' Alive

Mental Skill   Energy regulation

Physical Skill   Hitting

Purpose   To improve players' ability to identify and regulate changes in energy when hitting in pressure situations by practicing breathing exercises between pitches

Implementation   Position a flat hitting screen approximately 10 to 15 feet from home plate. From behind the screen, a tosser throws underhand pitches at varied speeds and locations. Before each pitch, the hitter steps out of the box and performs a centered breathing exercise: Breathe in slowly through the nose into the abdomen. Hold the breath for three seconds. Completely exhale through the mouth. The hitter attempts to "stay alive" at the plate by making solid contact with 20 pitches before making 5 hitting mistakes. The hitter keeps track of the number of times she makes solid contact with the ball, and the tosser keeps track of the number of times the hitter makes a hitting mistake. (When the hitter reaches 5 mistakes or 20 hits, the hitter and tosser should switch places.) Mistakes include

- swinging at bad pitches,
- not swinging at strikes,
- missing the ball,
- popping up, and
- failing to perform the breathing exercise.

Scoring　Keep track of the number of successful hits before reaching 5 mistakes.

Coaching Tip　Encourage hitters to be patient, to swing at good pitches, and to take the time to perform the breathing exercise. (To accommodate the needs of each player, the breathing exercise in this drill can be modified or replaced by any of the energy-regulating strategies described in chapter 1.)

2　*Pressure Ball*

Mental Skill　Energy regulation

Physical Skill　Hitting

Purpose　To help hitters learn to regulate energy levels when instructed by the coach to perform a specific task

Implementation　Two players take turns hitting against live pitching, rotating after each at-bat. Each player gets five at-bats. For each at-bat, the coach provides the hitter with a specific game situation. Here are some examples:

- Runner on second, no outs
- Runner on first, no outs
- Runner on third, one out
- Two strikes, runner on third, tie game

The hitter is expected to execute a correct response to each situation. This may include executing a bunt, hitting a sacrifice fly, looking for a particular pitch to hit to a specific location, and so forth. In between pitches, the hitter should step out of the box and check her energy level:

- If underaroused, the hitter should perform 5 to 10 high knee lifts.
- If overaroused, the hitter should do focus breathing: Breathe in through the nose, counting to three. Pause, holding the breath. Breathe out through the mouth, counting to three.

Scoring Hitters count the number of successful at-bats.

Coaching Tips

- Perform the drill on the field or in a batting cage.
- Use this drill to practice game strategies by requiring hitters to determine the correct response to various situations.
- You can also provide hitters with a specific task, such as hitting the ball to the right side of the field to move a runner from second to third base.

Variation To make the drill more gamelike, incorporate a defensive unit and base runners.

3 *Muscle Tension Awareness*

Mental Skill Energy regulation

Physical Skill Hitting

Purpose To develop players' kinesthetic awareness of muscle tension while performing proper hitting mechanics (this awareness may improve bat speed, reaction time, and accuracy)

Implementation Each hitter hits a total of 20 balls off of a tee. Instruct hitters to begin the drill with an extensive amount of muscle tension in the upper body, arms, forearms, hands, and wrists. Hitters should closely monitor and incrementally release a little tension after each swing. This procedure continues for the first 10 swings to determine the most relaxed, but appropriate level of muscle tension for optimal batting performance. Hitters should reach their optimal level of muscle tension on the 10th swing. At this point, players should have experienced 10 different levels of muscle tension. Hitters perform their last 10 swings at the same level of muscle tension experienced on the 10th swing.

Coaching Tips   Remind players that releasing muscle tension does not mean changing hitting mechanics (some of the best swings feel effortless). This drill is particularly helpful when players are too tense, frustrated, or trying too hard to get a hit.

4   *Mastering Your Muscle Tension*

Mental Skill   Energy regulation

Physical Skill   Hitting

Purpose   To improve muscle tension awareness by tensing and relaxing specific muscle groups while practicing basic hitting mechanics

Implementation   Each hitter performs 20 to 25 swings off of a tee. Before hitting, each hitter identifies a specific muscle group or body area that becomes tense when hitting (hands, forearms, shoulders, abdominals, quadriceps, hamstrings, and so forth). Before each swing, the hitter tenses that specific muscle group or body area for three seconds, then relaxes it for three seconds; the hitter repeats this procedure three times. A hitter should continue to tense and relax the targeted muscle group before each swing until she experiences relaxation in that area.

Coaching Tips
- This drill is good for those who tend to grip the bat very tightly, which limits the speed of the bat.
- Repeat this drill over time, targeting different muscle groups that are tense when hitting.

CONCENTRATION

Once a hitter has developed the ability to control her emotional responses and to maintain an optimal energy level for performance, she will be able to focus more clearly on executing at the plate. Effective concentration depends on what the hitter is focusing on and how long she can maintain her focus. A hitter will become her own worst enemy if she approaches the plate thinking about a previous performance or the consequences of not getting a hit. A hitter who develops the ability to concentrate on the right things at the right time with minimal effort will be more successful at accomplishing her performance goals.

Attention Style

As noted in chapter 1, some situations require a broad attention style (paying attention to many cues) and others require a narrow attention style (focusing on one or two cues). To achieve success, a hitter must be able to focus her attention on the most relevant cues and appropriately shift her attention at the right time to meet the demands of the task, in this case hitting the ball. When a hitter first approaches the plate, she should be paying attention to a variety of environmental cues to gather information about the situation. For example, she may check for runners on base, observe how the defense is positioned, and look to her coach for the signs. This represents a broad external attention style. Once the hitter steps into the batter's box, her attention will shift to the pitcher. As the pitcher begins her windup, the batter should be focused on the pitcher's release point to begin tracking the ball. When the hitter is devoting all of her attention to the ball, she is using a narrow external attention style.

Whether you're on deck or in the batting circle, by devoting your attention to the ball, you have the best chance for a good hit.

Most hitters do not think about the importance of shifting attention because it is a natural occurrence in everyday life. The situations that people are confronted with on a daily basis require them to shift their attention at different times and in different ways throughout the day. In contrast, a hitter should shift her attention in the same sequence for every at-bat in order to achieve consistency. To do this, a hitter must recognize the most suitable attention style for each aspect of hitting. Drill 5: From Here to There challenges players to efficiently shift attention from broad external to narrow external while hitting. By gaining an awareness of attention styles in practice, players will be able to shift at appropriate times and maintain focus on relevant cues during games.

Cues

A number of internal and external factors can potentially disrupt a hitter's ability to concentrate. Internal factors may include self-doubts, a desire to please a coach, or negative thoughts about a previous at-bat. External factors may include poor weather conditions, a bad call by an umpire, or obnoxious fans who will do anything to get into a batter's head. To concentrate effectively, a hitter must block out any factors that are not related to her performance. She must clear her mind by focusing on the present, on what she is going to do right now, rather than on what she has done in the past or what she might do in the future. Self-talk in the form of cue words, phrases, or short statements can assist hitters in blocking out unnecessary distractions. When two people are talking simultaneously, it is impossible to comprehend what both are saying. Therefore, if a hitter steps into the batter's box and repeats a phrase to herself such as "See the ball," her attention will be directed toward performing the task. Distractions that may hinder her ability to perform the task successfully will be blocked. In drill 6: Deaf to Distractions, a variety of distractions are created, and the hitter must use self-talk to direct her focus toward the task of hitting.

Hitters can also use cue words as triggers to initiate or stop an action. Hitting requires a quick decision followed instantaneously by a timely response. Once the hitter decides whether or not the pitch is good enough to hit, she can use a trigger word such as "yes" or "no" to influence the correct physical response. Drill 7: Cuts and Cues and drill 8: High Low Toss teach hitters to use trigger words to help reduce hesitation and improve reaction time.

Pitch Recognition

Once a hitter is in her stance and the pitcher begins her motion, the hitter must use a narrow external attention style. At this point, all of the hitter's attention should be focused on tracking the ball. To begin focusing on the ball, the hitter's attention should be directed at the pitcher's release point.

After a player learns to pay attention to the right cues at the right time, she can increase the intensity and duration of her focus. The better she becomes at focusing on one cue for a sustained period of time without being distracted, the more likely it is that she will be able to direct her attention to the ball when in the batter's box. A player can have great mechanics, but if she doesn't see the ball, she won't be able to hit it. Most hitters will track the ball from the pitcher's release, but not many hitters will actually see the ball contact the bat. Most hitters take their eyes off the ball a split second before it reaches the plate, which forces them to rely on their experience and kinesthetic awareness to make contact. Players who possess tremendous athletic ability can get away with this and still achieve a fair amount of success at the plate. But why settle for mediocre? If the pitcher is effective, and the ball is breaking at the moment the hitter takes her eyes off it, the hitter is likely to swing and miss or to hit a slow grounder, foul ball, or pop-up. But if a hitter is disciplined at the plate, and she continues to focus her attention on the ball until she actually sees it make contact with the bat, how can she miss?

Watching the ball until the point of contact is challenging, but recognizing the type of pitch being thrown is even more difficult. A batter who can consistently track the ball to the point of contact, can then develop the ability to identify the type of pitch that is being thrown. To do this, the hitter must determine the direction that the ball is spinning. For example, if the seams are rotating from bottom to top, the hitter can expect the ball to rise; if the seams are rotating from top to bottom, she can expect the ball to drop. The more information a hitter uses to decide on whether or not to swing at particular pitches, the better she will perform at the plate. In drill 9: Name That Pitch, hitters practice directing their focus exclusively on the ball and learn how to judge pitches without actually swinging the bat.

Hitting for Placement

Hitters need to be able to hit the ball to specified locations, and to do this, they must discipline themselves to be patient. A hitter should be looking for the ball to enter into a particular zone. When the hitter is ahead in the count, her zone should be small, toward the center of the plate, and she should be looking for "her" pitch. If the hitter falls behind in the count, she must expand this zone and look for any pitch that is close enough to make solid contact. Drill 10: Pick Your Pitch will help players develop the ability to hit particular pitches by maintaining focus on a contact point within the hitting zone.

There are many game situations in which a batter can benefit from the ability to hit the ball to particular locations on the field. For example, with less than two outs and a runner on second, a hit to right field could generate a run or at least put a runner in better scoring position. Unfortunately, this is an extremely difficult task. For most hitters, it's a struggle to consistently make solid contact, let alone to try to hit the ball to a specific location. But when a hitter has disciplined her mind and developed the ability to narrow her focus on the ball, to recognize specific pitches, and to track the ball to the point of contact, she will have the necessary tools to hit for placement. To do this effectively, a hitter must recognize each pitch and patiently wait for the one that will allow her to accomplish her goal. For example, hitting to right field would require a right-handed hitter to hold her swing until she recognizes an outside pitch. Once hitters become proficient at recognizing pitches and making good decisions, drill 11: Closest to the Cone can be used to practice the skill of hitting for placement.

5 From Here to There

Mental Skill   Concentration

Physical Skill   Hitting

Purpose   To help hitters identify the attention styles used when hitting and to improve hitters' ability to focus and shift their attention from broad to narrow

Implementation   Each hitter performs 20 to 25 swings (hitting off a tee). The hitter's objective for each swing is to identify and effectively shift focus between two attention styles:

- *Broad external* should be used before an at-bat. A hitter will focus on many environmental cues (e.g., coaches, opposing team, fans, game situation).
- *Narrow external* should be used during an at-bat. A hitter will narrow her concentration by focusing solely on the ball.

When hitting off a tee, hitters should practice shifting attention by focusing on many cues (e.g., the screen or anything in the background) before swinging. Just before initiating the swing, players should shift attention, focusing only on the ball.

Coaching Tips

- To help hitters shift attention quickly from broad to narrow, encourage them to use a phrase such as "see ball" or help them create their own phrases.
- Hitters may also benefit from shifting focus to a specific point on the ball.

Variations

- This drill can work in a progression from simple to complex. Players begin practicing this skill on the tee, and then integrate it into soft toss, pitching machine, and live pitching drills.
- A scrimmage situation provides the most realistic opportunity to identify the relevant environmental cues players will focus on during actual games.

6 *Deaf to Distractions*

Mental Skill Concentration

Physical Skill Hitting

Purpose To develop players' ability to direct attention to the most relevant hitting cues (such as the pitcher's release, the ball, or the task) when performing under distracting circumstances

Implementation Players need a partner for this drill. Hitting off a tee, one partner takes 10 swings, using a cue word before each swing (e.g., "ball," "focus," "hit," or "swing"). The same hitter then takes 10 more swings while her partner tries to distract her by humming, making funny gestures, or calling out various phrases such as "Don't swing!" "Watch out!" "Stop!" "You don't look right!" or "Where did you get those socks?" After each swing, the hitter reveals whether or not the chatter distracted her thoughts.

Scoring   Hitters keep track of the number of swings performed without being distracted. A 10 is a perfect score!

Coaching Tips

- Players will likely devise creative methods for distracting teammates, but you should encourage them to use gamelike taunting.
- Emphasize the importance of self-talk as a method for directing attention and maintaining focus.

7   Cuts and Cues

Mental Skill   Concentration

Physical Skill   Hitting

Purpose   To improve concentration and reaction time by allowing hitters to practice using cue words to initiate action

Implementation   Players need a partner for this drill. Each hitter will perform 15 to 20 swings. The hitter positions herself in alignment with home plate. The feeder stands on a bucket, positioned on the opposite side of the plate so that when her arm is extended it reaches out over the plate. She holds a tennis ball in her hand, palm down, extended over the plate. The feeder makes an initial upward movement to allow the batter time to stride, and then drops the ball. The hitter uses a trigger word (such as "ball," "hit," or "now") just before contact to help initiate a quick reaction to get her hands through the zone.

Scoring   Each hitter counts the number of times she makes solid contact with the ball.

Variations

- To increase the difficulty, use golf-ball-size Wiffle balls instead of tennis balls.
- To decrease the difficulty, allow the tennis balls to bounce one time before the hitter swings the bat.

8   High Low Toss

Mental Skill   Concentration

Physical Skill   Hitting

Purpose To improve concentration and decrease reaction time by forcing hitters to make quick decisions and initiate action with the help of cue words

Equipment Hitting screen (sock)

Implementation Players need a partner for this drill. Each hitter will perform 15 to 20 swings. The hitter positions herself in alignment with home plate so that she will hit the balls into a hitting screen. The feeder positions herself on the opposite side of the plate to perform a soft toss to the hitter. The feeder begins each toss with two balls in one hand, one ball between the thumb and index finger, and the other ball between the middle, ring, and pinkie fingers. When the feeder tosses the balls into the air, one should travel higher than the other; as she tosses, she will either say "high" or "low" to instruct the hitter which ball to hit. When the ball is tossed, the hitter will use a cue word (such as "ball," "focus," or "hit") to help initiate a quick reaction to get her hands through the zone.

Scoring Each hitter counts the number of times she makes solid contact with the ball.

Variation If players are unable to hold two balls in one hand, the drill can be modified to achieve the same results. The feeder can hold one ball in each hand. Instead of tossing two balls into the air, she can simulate a juggling motion, forcing the hitter to pay attention to both balls and to be prepared to hit the one that is tossed. The tosser will then decide when to release one of the balls. The hitter will respond by shifting her attention to the tossed ball, using her trigger word to initiate action, and swinging the bat.

9 *Name That Pitch*

Mental Skill Concentration

Physical Skill Hitting

Purpose To improve players' pitch selection and develop their ability to identify different types of pitches.

Implementation While a pitcher is warming up or practicing her mechanics, a hitter positions herself in the batter's box for a total of 20 pitches. The hitter does not swing at any pitches, but she judges whether each pitch is a ball or a strike by saying "no" or "yes" as the pitch crosses the plate. The hitter should use a narrow external attention style. The catcher determines the accuracy of the hitter's decision for each pitch. The catcher keeps track of the total number of pitches, and the hitter keeps track of the number of times she makes the correct judgment.

Scoring   Hitters count the number of successful reads out of 20.

Coaching Tip   Emphasize the importance of making the call loudly.

Variation   To increase the difficulty, instruct hitters to judge the type of pitch by recognizing the direction in which the seams are rotating.

10   Pick Your Pitch

Mental Skill   Concentration

Physical Skill   Hitting

Purpose   To improve players' pitch selection and develop their ability to hit particular pitches

Implementation   Each hitter will receive 5 swings or 15 to 20 pitches. Before each pitch, the hitter chooses a specific pitch location (e.g., inside, outside, high, low). The hitter focuses on holding her swing until a pitch is delivered to that specific location. The pitcher and catcher should mix up the pitches to avoid throwing the same pattern of pitches. After hitting a pitch thrown to the specified location, the hitter chooses a new location and repeats the drill.

Scoring   Hitters keep track of the number of swings taken at pitches in the correct location versus the total number of swings.

Coaching Tip   Remind hitters to focus on a contact point—the point at which the hitter wants her bat to meet the ball. If the ball is not pitched into this zone, the hitter should not swing at the pitch.

Variation   If hitters become effective at hitting pitches in particular locations, increase the difficulty by instructing hitters to swing only at specific pitches (e.g., rise, drop, curve, screw, change-up).

Coach Michelle Gromacki is a Division I head softball coach at California State University, Fullerton. In her four years as head coach, she has led her team to four consecutive Big West conference titles. Coach Gromacki contributes her favorite hitting drill, Center Toss, which helps to improve concentration by requiring players to differentiate between taking quality cuts and just going through the motions. Center Toss will also help hitters increase the intensity of their focus. Identifying the feeling associated with a high level of intense focus will provide hitters with information about the level of focus they should be applying for each at-bat during games.

Photo by Matt Brown®

Michelle Gromacki, head softball coach, California State University, Fullerton

Center Toss

Mental Skill   Concentration

Physical Skill   Hitting

Purpose   To prepare hitters for more successful at-bats by increasing the intensity of concentration for each pitch

Implementation   Players need a partner for this drill. Position a flat hitting screen approximately 20 feet from home plate. Each hitter will receive five at-bats, rotating with her partner after each at-bat. While the coach pitches to one hitter, the hitter's partner should remain in the on-deck circle. Hitters should be focused on swinging at good pitches and making the best contact possible for each at-bat. The object is to get a solid hit for each at-bat.

Scoring   Players keep track of the number of times they make solid contact with the ball. Count a point for each time the player makes solid contact; deduct a point each time the player swings at a bad pitch. A player's goal is a perfect score of five.

(continued)

Coaching Tips

- Be sure that the on-deck hitter is not just standing around. She should be making adjustments from her previous at-bat.
- When using the variation of this drill, instruct the hitters that the level of focus directed toward a single pitch should be the same level of focus applied for each pitch during an entire at-bat.

Variation   Perform the same drill, but require the players to rotate after each pitch. Each player should get a total of 10 to 15 pitches. A player should be ready to swing if the pitch is a strike, but if the pitch is a ball, she should hold her swing. Allowing only one pitch at a time forces players to increase the intensity of their concentration. The coach should emphasize aggressiveness and discipline at the plate.

11   *Closest to the Cone*

Mental Skill   Concentration

Physical Skill   Hitting

Purpose   To simulate pressure situations by requiring hitters to strategically place the ball

Implementation   Players need a partner for this drill. Strategically place brightly colored cones in the outfield. Hitters will get one at-bat for every cone (against live pitching). The partners compete with each other to see who can hit the ball closer to a targeted cone. To hit to specified cones, hitters must identify particular pitches. To identify certain pitches, hitters should create a phrase that will help them focus on the pitch they are looking for (such as "inside only" or "outside, outside"). For each at-bat, the hitter who places the ball closest to the targeted cone receives a point.

Scoring   The hitter who scores the most points is the winner.

Variation   Provide the hitters with realistic game situations before each at-bat. This will require hitters to think strategically and hit the ball to specific locations on the field depending on the demands of the situation.

CONFIDENCE

When a hitter steps into the batter's box, she is in a situation that is different from most sporting events. In most sports, an equal number of players compete against each other the entire time. But when a hitter steps up to the plate in softball, she is on the field all by herself competing against nine opponents. Although most hitters never consciously think about it (because it's the nature of the game), this could be very frightening for a hitter and could have detrimental effects on her confidence.

If a player learns to manage her arousal and concentrate effectively, she will be able to perform at a high level more consistently. And if she continues to experience success, her accomplishments will substantially increase her confidence. A player who continually fails to get a hit when runners are in scoring position may develop the belief that she does not have the ability to execute in clutch situations. Eventually, she will experience anxiety each time she approaches the plate under these circumstances, and her beliefs will negatively affect her performance. Fortunately, one bout of success is sometimes enough to prove to a player that she has the talent and ability to perform in any situation. If a player knows she is good at performing both the mental and physical aspects of hitting, she will be confident in her ability to execute at the plate under any circumstance.

A player should think of herself as a hitter from the moment she leaves the dugout to the time she returns. During a game, when a player enters the on-deck circle, she has time to prepare for her next at-bat. The way players prepare themselves in the on-deck circle often influences the outcome of their performance. Some hitters enter the circle with a competitive look that shows they are going to be a challenge for the pitcher. They walk with an air of confidence—head high, shoulders back, and a competitive spark in their eyes. Other hitters enter the circle looking as though they have failed before they even step into the batter's box. Their posture is hunched, their head is hanging down, and their feet drag across the dirt as they approach the plate. A pitcher who observes this type of behavior will be fueled by the look of fear or doubt in the hitter's eyes. An intuitive pitcher will know if she has the upper hand on a batter and will be able to detect if the hitter is feeling nervous. Unfortunately, many hitters don't realize how they look while they are playing. Their posture, body language, and mannerisms may be sending messages that contrast with how they truly think and feel. A confident hitter who walks with poise will be much more intimidating to her opponents than the confident hitter who shuffles to the plate. This is why it is important for players to work on their composure during practice and carry that attitude into competition.

When players are in between repetitions or waiting to hit during practice, many will use this time to relax or converse with teammates. Thus, when they step up to the tee or into the batter's box, they have not prepared to hit in the same manner they would prepare during a game. Periods of downtime, when players are not directly engaged in physical activity, provide the best opportunities to practice the mental aspects of hitting. Instead of tuning out, players could be practicing the skills necessary to give them the edge on their opponents. Drill 12: The Three Cs is a drill in which hitters can practice using the time in between at-bats to develop a competitive, intimidating presence.

Approaching the plate with a composed, confident attitude gives notice to the pitcher that the hitter intends to battle for a hit. This attitude sets the stage for the hitter to be the dominant player in the duel. Getting ahead in the count and forcing the pitcher to throw something down the center of the plate is a great feeling. However, there are going to be times when a hitter falls behind in the count and must work hard to protect the plate. It is at this time that a hitter must trust what she sees and be confident that she can make something happen. In this situation, a hitter must expand her strike zone and change her mind-set from looking for the perfect pitch to looking for anything close. How players think and feel at a given moment greatly influences their actions. If a hitter falls behind in the count and thinks, *Oh shoot, she's ahead of me. Don't chase a bad one*, she is setting herself up for failure. In contrast, a hitter who thinks, *I can do this, anything close and I'll blast it*, will most likely increase her chances for success. Drill 13: Protect the Plate enables players to practice using positive affirmations to prepare for hitting when behind in the count. Players often underestimate the power that thoughts, beliefs, and attitudes can have on performance. Positive affirmations can help reinforce a hitter's belief that she can and will make something happen. See figure 3.1 to learn a simple mental imaging exercise that can be used to demonstrate the extent to which the mind influences the body.

Figure 3.1   Mind–Body Connection

A mental imagery exercise that will demonstrate the power of the mind over physical movement is presented here. To prepare for this exercise, attach a paper clip to a 12-inch piece of string. Give this tool to each player. Then instruct each player to follow this series of instructions.

Position your elbow on a stable item (desktop or table) and hold the string between your thumb and forefinger, allowing the paper clip to dangle about half an inch above the surface.

Sit comfortably and close your eyes.

Imagine that the paper clip is moving to the left and right; think this thought for about 30 seconds; do not move your hand; open your eyes and see if the paper clip is moving in that direction.

Imagine that the paper clip is moving clockwise in a circle; think this thought for about 30 seconds; do not move your hand; open your eyes and see if the paper clip is moving in that direction.

Imagine that the paper clip is moving counterclockwise in a circle; think this thought for about 30 seconds; do not move your hand; open your eyes and see if the paper clip is moving in that direction.

Discuss the results with the players. Note that the mind is so powerful that when you concentrate on a thought, it actually has the capability to generate low-level nerve impulses that cause the body to respond to the thought. This demonstrates the impact mental thoughts have on physical performance.

12   *The Three Cs*

Mental Skill   Confidence

Physical Skill   Hitting

Purpose   To help players develop the three Cs (confidence, composure, competitiveness) by modeling confident behavior during live batting practice

Implementation   Players need a partner for this drill. Each hitter will get four or five at-bats against live pitching. While one partner is batting, the other partner is mentally and physically preparing for her next at-bat by modeling the three Cs in the on-deck circle. Players must exude confidence through body language, such as good posture, shoulders back, head high, and eyes focused on the pitcher. Don't allow players to drag their feet or head. Encourage players to develop a "love to hit, ready to hit, going to get a hit" attitude.

Coaching Tip Emphasize how looking defeated breeds failure and looking confident breeds success. This drill provides a perfect opportunity to film the players. Sometimes players don't realize what they look like when they are performing a skill. Filming will allow them to see what they look like and decide if they are presenting themselves in the manner in which they want to appear. Although this drill addresses the three Cs directly, you should emphasize to your players the importance of demonstrating a competitive, confident, and composed demeanor for every drill.

13 Protect the Plate

Mental Skill Confidence

Physical Skill Hitting

Purpose To practice using positive affirmations to improve players' confidence in their ability to make solid contact at the plate when behind in the count

Implementation Players need a partner for this drill. Each hitter will get four or five at-bats against live pitching, rotating with her partner after each at-bat. Each at-bat starts with an 0-2 count (no balls, two strikes). Hitters try to protect the plate by expanding the strike zone and looking to make contact. Before each at-bat, hitters should repeat a positive affirmation to themselves, such as "This pitch is mine," "See the ball," "I'm better than her," or "I own the box." Pitchers should work on throwing pitches to both corners of the plate.

Scoring Hitters count the number of successful at-bats.

Coaching Tips
- Encourage players to be aggressive at the plate.
- Instruct players on how to create positive affirmations that are customized to address their individual needs.

MENTAL IMAGERY

Mental imagery is a performance-enhancing strategy that can be implemented in a variety of ways. It can be used for problem solving, coping with injury, regulating energy, building confidence, improving concentration, and practicing physical skills. For example, a hitter may improve her hitting confidence by imagining herself successfully hitting the ball in an intense game situation. As noted in chapter 1, there are two types of imagery, internal and external; either one can positively influence performance. However, external imagery is generally easier to learn, but internal imagery is typically more effective.

The first step in learning how to use imagery is developing the ability to create a specific picture in the mind. The easiest way to develop a picture in the mind is to actually see the image in real life. Thoughts are often accompanied by a mental picture. When people think of an object that they see on a daily basis, such as a pencil, they automatically create a picture of that object in their mind because they know exactly what it looks like. People who are good at creating mental images may even sense what the object smells, tastes, and feels like. In contrast, a person rarely gets opportunities to observe how she acts in her environment, so it is difficult to create mental images of how she looks and behaves in various situations. For a hitter to be able to imagine herself swinging the bat from an external point of view, she must have a good idea of what she looks like when performing this skill. Many coaches use video equipment to provide feedback that will help hitters correct flaws in technique and refine hitting mechanics. When a hitter is able to watch herself on film, this provides an image she can re-create in her mind. However, videotaping is time consuming and requires expensive equipment. Another way for a player to develop this image is by practicing her swing in front of a mirror. This not only reflects her image, but also allows for to see herself and instantly analyze her mistakes in order to make adjustments while she is performing the skill. Drill 14: Mirror, Mirror, Where's the Ball? provides a method of teaching imagery from an external vantage point.

Once the player has developed the ability to create mental images of herself from an external point of view, the next step is imagining herself performing from an internal perspective. This is when she sees her performance through her own eyes as if she were actually performing. Often, players who are struggling at the plate will continually adjust their body position, stance, arms, grip, or bat angle in search of a quick fix. They make these adjustments but are not exactly sure what they look like because it is difficult for players to feel what they do when performing a skill. So they feel uncomfortable and don't know how to correct it. Players can change their physical positioning, but hitting truly comes from within. If a hitter knows what a good swing feels like and can see herself performing it correctly, she will be able to do it when she is actually hitting the ball. Drill 15: Eyes Wide Shut requires players to close their eyes and hit the ball. Without visual cues, other senses become more keen and players develop an awareness for how they feel when performing the skill (instead of solely concentrating on seeing the ball).

Players constantly worry about how hard or where the ball is hit rather than their hitting technique. As noted in the description of the principles of performance excellence, players should focus on the process rather than the outcome in order to reinforce correct technique and ensure they stay in the moment. When players succeed, they often don't worry about whether or not they performed the skill correctly and they tend to go through the motions. The Eyes Wide Shut drill provides the player with an opportunity to practice her internal imagery and to become more familiar with how her body feels while performing each movement of the skill. It also enhances a player's ability to create mental images using her visual, kinesthetic, and auditory senses.

If a player develops the ability to control the outcome of her images, she can experience success in any situation. This ability is especially helpful for players who are struggling or are in a hitting slump. If a player continually performs incorrectly, she must imagine herself doing the skill correctly so that she does not reinforce her bad habits. If she controls her imagery so that she experiences success, her mental success will eventually transfer into physical success. Drill 16: Perfect Swing is designed to help hitters develop control over their images. In this drill, a player imagines a perfect swing after performing each physical swing.

Once a hitter develops the ability to control the outcome of her images, she can start creating various situations in her mind. She can imagine hitting off of a pitcher who she will be facing in an upcoming competition. Or she can imagine hitting certain pitches that she is having difficulty recognizing. She may create a different situation for each at-bat that she imagines. By imagining success in situations that she has been struggling in, a hitter will enhance her confidence when actually performing in those situations. Drill 17: Inside, Outside, Upside Down is designed to help hitters identify and hit pitches in certain locations, such as low and inside. When a hitter becomes proficient at imagining and hitting specified pitches, this drill can be adjusted to include hitting successfully in various situations created by the coach. The hitter can also imagine the entire situation (runners on base, the opposing team, and so forth), see herself perform successfully, and then actually step into the box and make the vision a reality.

A successful hitter is one who has mastered the mental and physical components of hitting and can control them during games. Regardless of the situation, a hitter should approach each at-bat with a consistent level of mental and physical preparedness. After acquiring the necessary mental skills that accompany the physical aspects of hitting, a performance routine that incorporates all of these skills can be used to consistently achieve an optimal state for performance. See figure 3.2 for a sample batting performance routine. Refer to figure 2.3 (page 37) for creating an individualized batting routine. Drill 18: Step Up to the Plate provides a framework that hitters can use to develop an individualized performance routine.

Figure 3.2   Batting Pre-performance Routine

Instructions: Pre-performance routines are important in developing performance consistency. Hitters can use this worksheet to create individualized pre-performance routines. There are two parts to completing this worksheet. First, list the factors that you consider at each phase of preparation. Second, for each of the three phases, identify a letter that will be included in an acronym to serve as your pre-performance routine reminder. The acronym BAT is used in this sample.

List the sequence of your thoughts and behaviors when you are doing the following:

Phase I: Prepare

Leaving the on-deck circle

Check the number of outs and runners on base

Look to the coach for the signs

Tap cleats with bat to show coach I got the signs

Review situation and decide what pitch to look for

> Phase I: **B**
> (be aware)

Phase II: Automate

Preparing to step into the batter's box

Act confident; look determined

Take two practice swings

Scan the field

Smooth the dirt in the box

Step into the box; left foot first

> Phase II: **A**
> (act confident)

Phase III: Execute

Preparing for a pitch

Set into stance

Focus eyes on the pitcher

Repeat to myself "See the ball"

> Phase III: **T**
> (take action)

14 *Mirror, Mirror, Where's the Ball?*

Mental Skill Mental imagery

Physical Skill Hitting

Purpose To help players learn how to use external mental imagery to improve hitting mechanics

Implementation Using correct hitting mechanics, hitters perform 20 to 25 swings in front of a mirror. After completing each swing, the hitter closes her eyes and imagines herself performing the swing as if she is watching herself on video.

Coaching Tip Ensure that hitters are patient between swings and that the swings in their mental images are performed in real time.

Variation When players develop the ability to see themselves swing without looking in the mirror, the drill can be performed with the players hitting off a tee. Before each swing, the players imagine themselves performing correct mechanics.

15 *Eyes Wide Shut*

Mental Skill Mental imagery

Physical Skill Hitting

Purpose To develop players' internal imaging abilities and kinesthetic awareness of the physical components of hitting

Implementation Each hitter will take 20 to 25 swings off of a tee. The hitter performs every other swing with her eyes closed. While performing the blind swing, the hitter should imagine the situation as if her eyes are open; this will help her develop a kinesthetic awareness of how her body is actually moving throughout the swing. The hitter's partner looks for consistency in the hitter's mechanics (the swings with eyes closed should be consistent with the swings with eyes open). After 20 to 25 swings, the partners rotate.

Scoring Record the number of blind swings in which the hitter makes solid contact.

Coaching Tip Encourage hitters to go beyond just picturing their swing and to feel the actual movements of the swing while imagining themselves perform.

16   *Perfect Swing*

Mental Skill   Mental imagery

Physical Skill   Hitting

Purpose   To improve hitting mechanics by allowing players to mentally rehearse using images of successful hitting

Implementation   Each hitter will take 20 swings off of a tee. After each successful hit, meaning the player made solid contact with the ball, the hitter closes her eyes and imagines the exact same swing that she just performed. For optimal benefits, players must take the time to imagine the complete performance of each successful hit. After 20 swings, rotate to the next hitter.

Scoring   Record the number of solid hits out of a total of 20 chances.

Coaching Tips
- Instruct hitters to use either internal or external imagery depending on individual preference.
- Emphasize the importance of creating mental images in real time to make the images more realistic and effective.

Variation   When a player becomes proficient at re-creating successful images in her mind, she can perform this type of drill as a soft toss, pitching machine, or live pitching drill and even imagine specific pitches.

17   *Inside, Outside, Upside Down*

Mental Skill   Mental imagery

Physical Skill   Hitting

Purpose   To improve players' ability to identify and hit specific pitches with the help of mental imagery

Implementation   Each hitter chooses to hit only inside or only outside pitches (hitting against live pitching). If the hitter chooses to hit inside pitches, she should not swing unless the pitcher throws an inside pitch. Before each pitch, the hitter imagines herself swinging at the specified pitch. After 10 successful contacts with a correct pitch, rotate to the next hitter.

Coaching Tip   Ensure that hitters are patient between pitches and are creating mental images in real time.

18 *Step Up to the Plate*

Mental Skill   Energy regulation, concentration, confidence, imagery

Physical Skill   Hitting

Purpose   To develop a hitting routine that will mentally and physically prepare the batter to be more consistent and successful at the plate

Implementation   While pitchers are warming up or doing work in the bull pen, hitters stand in the batter's box for 15 to 25 pitches. The hitter enacts a gamelike batting stance, completely prepared to hit the ball, but does not swing at any of the pitches. After each pitch, the hitter steps out of the box and performs a prehit routine. The hitter's goal is consistency in her routine. Elements of a sample routine might include the following:

- Take two steps out of the box
- Look for signs
- Adjust helmet
- Take two practice swings
- Wipe down bat
- Look at the pitcher
- Smooth out dirt in the box
- Step back into the box
- Take one more practice swing
- Crouch into stance

Coaching Tip   Emphasize the importance of creating an individualized routine that is specific and used consistently in preparation for each pitch.

MENTAPHYSICAL WRAP-UP

A player with tremendous athletic ability may continually experience success regardless of whether she has correct hitting mechanics or sound mental toughness. Her success may be attributed to competing among players of a lower caliber of ability. For example, her swing may be long and loopy, but if she is facing a pitcher who is slow, she will be able to get the bat around in time to make solid contact with the ball. When she advances to the next level, she will most likely face pitchers who throw the ball at higher speeds, and her loopy swing will no longer be effective. Unfortunately, because she has experienced success with this swing for so many years, she may be reluctant to adjust and refine her skills. A lack of success may then lead to self-doubts about her ability to compete at this new level. Players who do not understand this concept may become frustrated with their performance and eventually drop out of the sport. Athletes must continually assess how they practice and prepare for competition, but more important, they must be willing to make the necessary adjustments to achieve success. Ultimately, becoming a great hitter is a choice that involves making a commitment to developing both the physical and mental skills needed for hitting—a commitment to the mentaphysical approach. Refer back to figure 2.3 (page 37) for a worksheet to create an individualized hitting routine.

4

Bunting

In general, fastpitch softball is a low scoring game, especially when two teams are competing with strong defensive units on the field and dominating pitchers in the circle. Some may even think of the game as a pitchers' duel. When equally matched, teams will battle back and forth, inning after inning—three up, three down—sometimes going into extra innings, and often resulting in a final score of 1-0, 2-1, or 3-2. Therefore, coaches and players are constantly exploring ways to create scoring opportunities. For this reason, bunting has become an effective offensive strategy that is used to advance runners into scoring position, to produce runs, or even to get safely to first base. Coaches are often willing to sacrifice outs to advance base runners. Bunting as a strategic tactic is often used during close, low scoring games. If a team is winning or losing by several runs, coaches are not likely to use bunting because generating one or two runs will not affect the outcome of the game.

Bunting can provide the hitting team with an extra offensive threat. The successful execution of a bunt could mean the difference between winning and losing a ball game. Although many coaches have invented creative variations and different names for the types of bunts, some of the most common types are the sacrifice, squeeze, drag (surprise), push, and slap. Because each bunt has a specific purpose, a player must be familiar with the strategic approach required to successfully perform each type of bunt.

The sacrifice bunt, for example, is the most well known and widely used type of bunt. The purpose of the sacrifice bunt is for the hitter to sacrifice her own at-bat to advance a runner from one base to the next. The at-bat typically results in an out at first base. This bunt is used when a runner is on first or second with less than two outs. In this situation, unlike regular hitting, the bunter must understand that her primary objective is to advance her teammate to the next base rather than to try to get safely to first. If, however, she advances the runner and makes it to first by beating the throw or by forcing an error on the defense, she has done her primary job successfully and also provided her team with an added advantage (saving an out and having an additional base runner). Unfortunately, a player might emphasize trying to get a base hit off of the bunt instead of moving the runner. For example, she may wait to square around until the last second or begin moving toward first base before she has successfully bunted the ball in fair territory. These behaviors typically cause the batter to fall behind in the count, bunt a foul ball, pop up, or miss completely. Not only does she make an out for her team, but she also fails to move the runner. In a sacrifice bunt situation, it is imperative that the hitter know and execute her primary role.

The push bunt is similar to the sacrifice in that the batter squares early, drawing the corner defensive players closer to the plate. In an attempt to put the ball past the defenders (instead of dropping the ball in front of the plate), the batter pushes her arms forward on contact to direct the ball with added velocity. While sacrifice and push bunts broadcast the bunt to the defense, other bunts such as the squeeze, drag, and slap offer an element of surprise. When performing these bunts, the batter attempts to mislead the defense by not showing her intent to bunt until just before contact.

There are numerous advantages for players who have the ability to perform a variety of bunts. It is challenging for the opponents to defend against a batter who can hit with power or lay down a surprise bunt on command. Bunting can also be effective for teams that are having trouble generating hits against good pitching. Bunting is an elemental component to any coach's strategic planning, and it is also one of the most basic, easiest parts of the game. When teaching bunting tactics, coaches should instruct hitters to be patient, stay calm, keep their eyes on the ball, and let the pitcher and ball do the work.

ENERGY REGULATION

Because a hitter is doing a specific job when bunting, her arousal levels may change depending on the type of bunt attempted. Players who are instructed to bunt may get nervous because they must accomplish a given task. To have the best chance of bunting successfully, a player must remain patient and calm in the batter's box. If a player is too anxious and shifts her weight forward in the box, she will decrease her ability to see and react to the ball. Therefore, it is important to remain composed while performing this skill. Drill 19: Loose Bunting challenges the hitter to regulate her energy level while bunting in a pressure situation.

Attempting to execute a squeeze bunt will likely cause changes in energy, typically increasing the batter's level of arousal. A squeeze bunt is unique in that it requires a mind-set that forces the batter to go against everything she has disciplined herself to do at the plate. Although she has trained her mind and body to only swing at good pitches, she must make an attempt to bunt the ball regardless of where it is thrown. The element of surprise is very important when executing a squeeze bunt. If the batter allows this situation to cause overexcitement, she may square around too early and telegraph her intent to the defense. If the fielders know that a squeeze play is on, they will immediately charge the plate, and the runner at third will likely be out. Drill 20: Executing the Squeeze will teach players how to identify and regulate energy while performing a squeeze play.

19 Loose Bunting

Mental Skill Energy regulation

Physical Skill Bunting

Purpose To improve players' ability to identify and regulate energy when bunting under pressure

Implementation Players need a partner for this drill. Each bunter will get two opportunities to lay down a bunt (off of a pitching machine). Before each bunt attempt, the hitter will step out of the batter's box and perform a circle breathing exercise: Slowly take a deep abdominal breath through the nose for four seconds. Hold the breath for four seconds. Slowly exhale through the mouth for four seconds. During the exhaling phase, relax the shoulders so that they actually lower. Partners rotate after two bunt attempts or one successful bunt. Complete 10 repetitions of the drill.

Scoring Keep track of the number of successful bunts out of the total number of attempts.

Coaching Tips
- Teach the players how to perform a circle breathing exercise before implementing this drill.
- To make the drill more realistic, instruct the feeder to adjust the pitching machine to throw varied pitches.

Variation When players become proficient at performing circle breathing, it can be used in live pitching drills.

20 Executing the Squeeze

Mental Skill Energy regulation

Physical Skill Bunting

Purpose To improve players' ability to regulate energy when bunting in a pressure situation

Implementation   Form two bunting teams to compete against each other. (Live pitching is used in this drill.) Instruct the pitcher to throw good, average, and bad pitches. Rotating back and forth between teams, each bunter will receive one pitch to lay down a squeeze bunt. Players should relax the shoulder muscles by consciously tensing and relaxing the shoulders before stepping into the batter's box; this will allow for more controlled and coordinated movements, which will increase the likelihood of laying down a successful bunt.

Scoring   The first team to perform 10 successful squeeze bunts wins.

Coaching Tips

- Remind the players to get into a mind-set in which they will attempt to bunt the ball regardless of where it is pitched.
- Remind bunters to wait until the last second to square around because the squeeze play is supposed to surprise the defense.

Variation   Try the Bunting Game. One bunting team is on defense and a pitcher is in the pitcher's circle. Similar to an actual game, teams will compete for five to seven innings. Start each inning with a runner on first base. Allow the bunting team to use any type of bunt; hitting away or taking a full cut will result in an out. Teams are awarded one point each time they successfully advance a runner and two points if a runner scores. When the game is complete, the team with the most points wins.

CONCENTRATION

With the exception of the squeeze bunt, players must wait for a good pitch when bunting. If the hitter tries to bunt a bad pitch, she is not likely to bunt the ball in fair territory or to advance a base runner. Although a sacrifice bunt is designed to give the batter up, this does not mean that the batter should make it easy on the defense by bunting the ball directly to an infielder. Advancing a runner is the primary objective, but a batter should also challenge the defense. Therefore, if one fielder charges hard, the hitter should try to bunt the ball in the opposite direction. If both fielders are playing aggressively, clearly expecting the bunt and charging the plate, the hitter can make the quick decision to change to a push or a slap bunt in an attempt to get the ball past the corners and the pitcher. This can be particularly effective when there is a runner on first and the shortstop is cheating toward second base to cover the steal. The ball can then be pushed through the gap between the third-base player and the pitcher. Drill 21: Stripes or No Stripes helps the hitter focus on the ball while practicing bunting to different sides of the field. This drill uses striped balls. Instructions for making striped balls can be found in figure 4.1.

Focusing on the ball requires a narrow external attention style, but being an effective bunter during games may require a player to quickly shift her attention from broad external to narrow external. If a player can concentrate effectively enough to recognize how the defense is moving while the pitch is being delivered, she can adjust and use the tactic that is most likely to get the job done. Drill 22: Getting It Done challenges the hitter to adjust her attention quickly from reading the defense to preparing for the pitch.

Figure 4.1   Creating Striped Balls

Striped balls can be used for several offensive and defensive drills. By forcing players to keep their focus on the ball, these drills improve the intensity and duration of player concentration. Stripes are used instead of colors because the number of stripes on each ball can represent the bases. Several drills in this book integrate the striped ball concept, and coaches should feel free to use this idea to create their own innovative striped ball drills.

To create striped balls you will need:

1. Permanent marker or black spray paint to create the black lines on each ball. If you decide to use paint, you should tape off the areas on each ball that you do not want to get painted, and then spray the ball.

2. Be sure that the lines are far apart and thick enough so that players can easily differentiate between two stripes and three stripes when the ball is rotating.

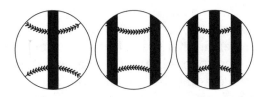

21   *Stripes or No Stripes*

Mental Skill   Concentration

Physical Skill   Bunting

Purpose   To enhance players' concentration and improve their ability to make quick decisions regarding bunt placement

Implementation   Set up a pitching machine on the field or in a batting cage. Mark half of the machine balls with stripes. Each bunter will receive 20 to 25 pitches. Instruct the players to bunt to a particular location; for example, if the ball is striped, bunt the ball down the third-base line, and if the ball is not striped, bunt the ball down the first-base line.

Coaching Tip   To increase the difficulty, use the number of stripes to represent various types of bunts.

22   *Getting It Done*

Mental Skill   Concentration

Physical Skill   Bunting

Purpose   To help players practice shifting their attention from broad external to narrow external by first recognizing the positioning and movement of the defense and then fixating on the ball

Implementation   Position defensive players at first and third base. Each bunter will receive 10 pitches off of a pitching machine. The coach stands in a position that cannot be seen by the bunter. Before each pitch, the coach gives a sign to the defensive players using one finger, three fingers, or a fist. If the coach holds up one finger, the first-base player will charge the plate while the third-base player slowly creeps in. If the coach holds up three fingers, the third-base player will charge the plate while the first-base player slowly creeps in. As the pitch approaches the plate, the bunter must read the defense and then bunt the ball away from the player who is charging. If the coach signals a fist, both fielders charge, and the bunter should execute a push bunt or pull back and slap the ball.

Scoring   Hitters receive one point for each successful bunt.

Coaching Tip   Instruct the defenders to move as soon as the ball leaves the pitching machine; movements should be realistic, and players should play aggressively when charging the ball.

Variation   Position an additional defensive player at first base. This player stays at first base and covers the bag (she does not charge the plate). This allows the first- and third-base players to complete each play by fielding the bunt and throwing to first base.

Photo courtesy of UC Davis Athletic Media Relations

University of California at Davis coaching staff

Coach Kathy DeYoung has been with the University of California at Davis for 25 years. In the spring of 2003, the Aggies won their first Division II national championship and are now in the process of moving to Division I status. First assistant Mieko Nagata shares her favorite bunting drill, Balanced Bunting, which forces players to maximize their concentration. It does this by requiring players to alter their bunting position, increasing the difficulty of the task.

Balanced Bunting

Mental Skill   Concentration

Physical Skill   Bunting

Purpose   To challenge hitters to focus on bunt execution while balancing on one foot and using only one hand (this helps players identify common bunting errors and make corrections)

Implementation   Each bunter will bunt 8 to 10 pitches from a pitching machine or front toss. Bunters position themselves by balancing on one foot (their nondominant foot). Bunters are also required to use only their dominant hand to execute the bunt; they may use a couple of fingers on their nondominant hand to balance the bat if needed. Encourage the hitters to focus on their technique and to use proper mechanics while executing the bunt.

Coaching Tips   This drill only works if bunters use a pivot bunt instead of squaring to the pitcher.

Variation   To increase the complexity, use tennis balls. Bounce the balls so that players must pay attention to the height of the ball on contact in order to get the bat on top of the ball.

CONFIDENCE

When a player is frustrated with her hitting, bunting can be used to provide a boost of confidence. If a hitter consistently swings and misses, switching to a bunt will simplify the task by giving her more time to focus. Bunting eliminates the challenge of trying to make contact between two moving objects and increases the likelihood of making contact with the ball. If a hitter makes contact with the ball through bunting, this may provide her with the confidence she needs to hit away later in the game. If she is struggling at the plate because she has been in a hitting slump or because the pitcher is hot, a drag bunt can also be used to generate a base hit. Drill 23: Bunt in the Box is a drill created to develop confidence in the ability to control the placement of bunts. If a player can master this drill, she will at least have confidence in her bunting abilities, and this will give her an additional strategic tool to use at the plate.

23 *Bunt in the Box*

Mental Skill   Confidence

Physical Skill   Bunting

Purpose   To increase players' confidence in their ability to control bunt placement

Implementation   Each bunter will receive 15 pitches from a tosser located 15-20 feet away. Position bunting targets (cones) in strategic locations on the field in front of home plate (target placement may vary depending on coach preference). Before each pitch, designate a location for the ball to be bunted.

Scoring   Keep track of the number of successful bunts out of the total number of bunt attempts.

Variation   When hitters gain confidence in their bunt placement abilities, perform this drill using a pitching machine or live pitching.

MENTAL IMAGERY

Bunting, like any other skill, requires specific technical precision. It is up to the coach to determine which type of bunting techniques will be used by a team. Regardless of style, a player must practice her bunting mechanics to become a successful bunter. Mental imagery, such as the strategy proposed in drill 24: Basic Bunting Imagery, can be used to reinforce bunting techniques and to help players learn variations and different types of bunts.

24 *Basic Bunting Imagery*

Mental Skill Mental imagery

Physical Skill Bunting

Purpose To improve players' bunting techniques through the use of mental imagery

Implementation Players perform correct bunting mechanics in front of a mirror. After viewing her bunting technique, the player closes her eyes and imagines herself performing a bunt as if she is watching herself on video. Perform 15 to 20 repetitions.

Coaching Tip Ensure that players are patient in between bunts and that the bunts in their mental images are performed in real time.

Variations

- When players become proficient at creating mental images of correct bunting techniques, this drill can be performed using a pitching machine or live pitching. Before each bunt, the player should imagine herself performing correct mechanics.
- Before each pitch, the coach can also provide bunting situations such as "runner on first, no outs" or "runner on third, one out, squeeze situation." Before stepping into the batter's box, the bunter should imagine herself performing the correct response for each situation.

MENTAPHYSICAL WRAP-UP

A player should develop a pre-performance routine that accommodates any hitting situation. During this routine, she will mentally rehearse her objective so that she can execute any hitting skill, including the various types of bunts. To develop this routine, see the sample batting routine in figure 3.2 (page 71) and refer back to figure 2.3 (page 37) to create your own.

5

Baserunning

If you examine the sport of softball in depth, you can see that baserunning is a fundamental and important part of the game, but is rarely addressed directly. Great baserunning could mean breaking a tie or getting an extra run to cushion a lead. For most softball skills, players do better when they feel calm and relaxed. Baserunning, on the other hand, requires sudden bursts of energy. Sometimes practicing baserunning can be boring and strenuous, but players should keep in mind that if they are running the bases, it means they have succeeded at getting on base. Occupying bases allows teams to pose an offensive threat to the opposition. To do this effectively, base runners must be aggressive, consistent, and alert on every pitch.

There are many components of baserunning that make it a challenging task. Successful baserunning requires quick reaction time whether reacting to a hit or stealing a base. The physical demands of baserunning include coordinating the pitcher's release with an explosive jump off the base. Efficient baserunning also requires astute field awareness. Players must process signs, read the defense, determine the course of action, and respond to dynamic situations. Although coaches are positioned at first and third base to direct runners, each player must take responsibility for making correct strategic responses such as when to round a bag, when to advance on an overthrow, and when to slide to avoid a tag.

Developing the four targeted mental skills will help players optimize their baserunning. Clearly, energy regulation is important; the stop-and-start action of baserunning challenges players to adjust energy levels instantaneously and often. Concentration is also critical; the ability to pick up signs and quickly make the appropriate response is mandatory for executing an aggressive attack. Baserunning is an assertive skill. Base runners must literally jump at the chance to advance to another base. Confidence is a necessary ingredient to maximize baserunning opportunities; a player must trust that she has the capability to turn a single into a double or to steal a base. If a base runner doubts her ability and hesitates on the bases, she will be thrown out by the defense or forced back to the original base. Base runners are confronted with many situations that make this skill mentally challenging. Baserunning decisions must be made with split-second timing. Mental imagery provides athletes with another opportunity to rehearse various skills, situations, and outcomes. These psychological skills will allow a player to become more of an offensive threat on the bases, thus helping the team score runs—the ultimate objective in softball.

ENERGY REGULATION

The explosive power needed to make sudden movements requires players to exert enormous amounts of energy on command. This is particularly challenging when a player must transition from swinging the bat to getting out of the box. These movements are completely different. Hitting requires the production of force to manipulate an object (the bat), and running requires the generation of power to move the body. Performing this transition efficiently can make the difference between a hit or an out. Drill 25: Burst of Power will teach hitters to generate a surge of energy after making contact with the ball.

25 *Burst of Power*

Mental Skill   Energy regulation

Physical Skill   Baserunning

Purpose   To help players develop a burst of speed when leaving the batter's box

Implementation   Each player hits a ball off of a tee at home plate and then runs to first base. Instruct players to use a trigger word such as "go" or "now" to inspire a burst of power to get out of the box. Players say this trigger or activating word to themselves to increase energy when transitioning from swinging the bat to getting out of the box.

Variation   This drill can also be performed starting with a dry swing (no ball) at home plate or when hitting against live pitching. To make this drill more challenging, instruct players to use exaggerated sprinting motions (high knees) for at least 10 steps as they accelerate out of the box.

CONCENTRATION

Baserunning requires a type of concentration that is unique compared to other softball skills. Most skills require a player to focus broadly (on many cues) and then shift her attention to a narrow focus (one cue). For example, a hitter will first scan the field, paying attention to many factors, but when she steps into the batter's box, she will narrow her focus and hone in on the delivery of the pitch. Although a base runner must also scan the field and take into account many aspects of the situation, when she turns her attention to the delivery of the pitch, she must continue to sustain a broad field awareness. One mental lapse can affect a runner's ability to respond to a play. Drill 26: Wait for the Catch will teach base runners to direct and shift their attention according to the demands of the situation.

Another situation that requires astute concentration is when a base runner is sliding into a base during a close play. A player must be aware of the direction the ball is arriving from and the position of the defensive player who will be applying the tag. If a base runner can maneuver her body to get around the tag or stretch as far away from the tag as possible, she will increase her chances of being safe at the bag. During a game, a smart maneuver around a tag at the plate could mean the difference between scoring a run or being called out—and could therefore change the entire momentum of the game. Drill 27: Find the Bag emphasizes avoiding the tag when sliding into base.

26 Wait for the Catch

Mental Skill Concentration

Physical Skill Baserunning

Purpose To improve baserunning skills by requiring players to react to a variety of baserunning situations

Implementation Position base runners at any or all of the bases. The coach hits to the outfielders from home plate. Base runners must assess the situation and react appropriately when the ball is contacted. Runners should be taught to change their focus from broad (to analyze the situation) to narrow (as the pitch is being delivered), and then back to broad (when the ball crosses the plate).

27 Find the Bag

Mental Skill Concentration

Physical Skill Baserunning and sliding

Purpose To improve players' ability to avoid the tag when sliding into a base during a close play

Implementation Players line up at first base to take turns as the base runner. A shortstop gets into position to cover second base, and a pitcher delivers a pitch to the plate. On the delivery, the base runner attempts to steal second base. The catcher makes a throw to second, and the base runner tries to avoid the tag while sliding into the base.

Variation To decrease the difficulty, a coach can position herself between second base and the pitcher's circle to throw the ball to the shortstop (who will apply a tag at second base). The coach can rotate her position around second base so that throws will arrive from different angles. Base runners can also start from second base and practice avoiding a tag at third base. The coach can also hit to the outfielders, who will make plays on base runners advancing from home plate to second base, first base to third base, or second base to home plate.

CONFIDENCE

Base runners must trust in their ability to see the situation and to react instinctually. A hesitation on the bases will force a runner into an out or force her back to the original bag. A player's composure on the bases will influence how the defense reacts. If a base runner looks timid, the defense will not have to pay much attention to her. This will allow them to focus on other defensive demands. However, if a base runner is aggressive, the defense will have to be extra alert. Aggressive baserunning is more likely to distract defensive players from their primary focus and may provide the hitting team with an extra advantage. A base runner will pose more of a threat if she takes an aggressive lead on every pitch. If she does not take an aggressive lead until she is instructed to steal, the defense will know her intent and will make an easy out on the play. The best method for building confidence in any skill is to provide opportunities for success. Thus, coaches should create situations in practice where players experience improvement and gain confidence. Drill 28: Out of the Blocks is designed to improve baserunning by emphasizing the importance of efficient decision making.

28   *Out of the Blocks*

Mental Skill   Confidence

Physical Skill   Baserunning

Base runners must constantly be alert and full of confidence. A second's hesitation might cost you an out.

Purpose   To improve players' overall baserunning performance by practicing quick decision making on the bases and by enhancing cardiovascular fitness

Implementation   Form a line of base runners at home plate and instruct one base runner to occupy each base. The coach hits from home plate to various locations on the field. When the ball is contacted, each base runner must respond to the hit as if she is the only runner on the bases. After each play is complete, base runners rotate to the next base to start the following play (for example, if a runner starts at first base and advances to third on the play, she will return to second base before the next play). Outfielders can practice fielding the balls, but they should not make any plays; this will help base runners make their decisions.

Coaching Tip   Encourage correct tactical decisions. This will reinforce the players' confidence in their ability to accurately respond in game situations.

Variation   The coach can vary the number of outs or the game situation before each play.

Brian Kolze has been leading the University of the Pacific softball program for 11 years. He is the winningest coach in program history, establishing a prominent position for the program by earning the right to compete in four of the past five NCAA regional tournaments. The Tigers have also been ranked in the top 20 according to the National Fast Pitch Coaches Association for several seasons. Coach Kolze offers his favorite baserunning drill, Point of No Return. This drill improves players' confidence in their ability to take an aggressive lead while on base.

Brian Kolze, head coach, University of the Pacific

Photo courtesy of Pacific Athletic Media Relations

Point of No Return

Mental Skill Confidence

Physical Skill Baserunning

Purpose To challenge base runners to take an aggressive lead on fly balls to the outfield

Implementation Outfielders assume their primary positions; infielders are positioned at each base. Consider having the outfielders with the strongest arms take part in this drill. A base runner is positioned at first or second base (or both). The coach hits fly balls to the outfield. Runners are expected to take an aggressive lead. The goal is to determine how large a lead they can take and still get back to the original base if the ball is caught. If the ball is not caught, runners will be in a good position to advance at least one base and possibly two bases.

Coaching Tip If the ball is hit so deep that runners advance past the next base and the ball is caught, remind runners to cross back over that base before returning to the base where they started.

MENTAL IMAGERY

There are hundreds of possible scenarios that a base runner may face in softball. The decisions a base runner must make can be simple, such as stealing a base on a passed ball, or more complex, such as getting into a rundown between first and second when there is a runner on third base. Mental imagery training is known for being particularly effective for enhancing skills that are mentally complex. Baserunning decisions are a good example of this type of mental challenge. Drill 29: See the Speed is designed to help players use imagery to practice baserunning skills and strategy. A good time to implement this drill is when a coach wants the team to avoid fatigue—the day before a game or after an intense practice.

29 *See the Speed*

Mental Skill   Mental imagery

Physical Skill   Baserunning

Purpose   To practice responses to baserunning situations using mental imagery

Implementation   The players lie down and relax in a comfortable position in the outfield or a grassy area. The coach talks the players through various baserunning situations that may occur during a game. Create several examples, such as "You're a runner on first and there are no outs; a high fly ball is hit to left field . . . How do you respond?" Each player creates a mental image of herself responding to the situation. After each situation, discuss the correct response.

Coaching Tip   Describe the situations slowly to provide players with ample time to create the images in their minds.

MENTAPHYSICAL WRAP-UP

Although baserunning is undeniably a major factor in winning softball games, practicing baserunning is often considered boring. To develop performance excellence on the bags, a runner must master two distinct skills: the mental decision making necessary for quick and correct baserunning decisions and the physical energy burst necessary to sprint from one bag to another. Regardless of the situation, a runner must be ready to make decisions, or respond to a coach's decision, and run as fast as possible. Drill 30: See the Situation allows players to practice both of the major baserunning skills.

30　*See the Situation*

Mental Skill　Energy regulation, concentration, confidence, imagery

Physical Skill　Baserunning

Purpose　To practice quick decision making and develop players' instinctive baserunning ability

Implementation　The entire team lines up along the first-base line. One coach simulates a pitching motion from the pitcher's circle. While the pitching motion is being simulated, all base runners should take an aggressive gamelike lead as if preparing to run from first to second. During this time, the coach calls out a situation (e.g., "Fly ball to right field"). The players must process the information and react accordingly (e.g., players tag up). The coach observes the entire team to ensure that each player made the correct initial response, and then the coach provides further instruction (e.g., "Ball is caught"). Player responses may vary according to player speed and situation; when the coach reports that the ball has been caught, one player may decide to tag up and advance to the next base, while another player may decide to return to the original base.

Coaching Tip　Encourage correct tactical decisions. This will reinforce the players' confidence in their ability to accurately respond in game situations.

Variation　Practice various situations with players lined up as if they are a base runner at first, second, or third base.

6

Infield Defense

The infielders, including the first-, second-, and third-base players, as well as the shortstop, are primarily responsible for getting outs. This requires quick and precise fielding techniques to keep runners off of the bases or to limit their ability to advance. A team with a strong offense may be able to score runs, but if the team's defense is not strong enough to limit the offensive production of opponents, winning games can be quite difficult. An infielder must possess the basic ability to catch, field, and throw, but other physical skills and attributes (such as strength, agility, coordination, and reaction time) also contribute to adept fielding. A player will typically become specialized and proficient at an infield position that complements her physical strengths and abilities. For example, the demands at first base are best filled by a player who is tall, left-handed, catches well, and has good footwork at the base. In contrast, the qualities of a shortstop may include good fielding range, a strong and accurate arm, and effective communication skills.

The infielders must work as a cohesive unit. Although players have distinct roles and responsibilities that are completely independent of each other, achieving success requires interdependence among teammates. Each player has a specific base and area on the field that she is responsible for covering, but these areas overlap. Plays that occur in these overlapping regions require players to communicate well with one another. If players fail to communicate effectively, the field may seem larger than it actually is. By communicating verbally, nonverbally, and intuitively, players will get a sense of support from each other. This will tighten these gaps and offer the illusion that the field is not so large. When players are not engaged and connected, they will be more likely to play as individuals rather than team players. Although athletes do not have to be the best of friends in order to perform well together on the infield, it is true that people who like each other communicate with each other more effectively. So while getting along isn't an absolute requirement for optimal performance, it does make playing together more fun, efficient, and ultimately, easier.

Making a play on the infield requires an instinctive reaction and a quick decision, followed immediately by a controlled response (the player reacts to a hit by fielding the ball, deciding where to throw, and executing the play). For some players, playing defense is the most exciting part of the game, and for others it is the most boring. How involved an infielder is in the action may depend on her fielding position and the nature of a particular game. On any given day, an infielder may be involved in numerous infield plays or may never even get a chance to make a play. For example, in seven innings, a first-base player may execute 20 plays while a third-base player executes 1 or 2 plays. If a team has a very dominating pitcher, the number of plays may be limited for all infielders.

Every time a new batter approaches the plate, each infielder must process information and make adjustments according to the demands of the situation. Elements to consider include the batter's past performance, base runners, the number of outs, the inning, and the current game score. Although infielders may not be physically involved in each play, they must sustain focus during all game situations. The dynamics of the sport of softball create an atmosphere that is constantly in flux. Whether a player gets numerous opportunities to handle the ball during a game or only gets a few opportunities, she must be mentally and physically ready to perform when the time comes.

ENERGY REGULATION

Because of the varied nature of the game, an infielder must learn to control her energy throughout competition. Softball teams often play two or more games in a day. During the summer and even into the fall, some softball teams travel to tournaments where they play as many as seven games in one weekend! To consistently perform at a high caliber, a player must not allow her energy to fall below or rise above the most ideal level for performance. When gearing up for a game, a player may need to engage in mental or physical activities to increase her energy and get the competitive juices flowing (or to decrease her energy if she is feeling overexcited). Refer back to chapter 2 for a discussion regarding pre-performance routines. Players must also be able to make energy adjustments during games. Competition tends to create intense situations, and softball is no exception. Imagine the energy management required of an infielder when the bases are loaded with no outs. At this point, it would be helpful if she had specific strategies to keep herself calm and composed.

Managing Energy Level

To regulate energy, a player must be able to recognize when she is not operating at an optimal level. Toward the end of a game or competitive series, when players have been standing for long periods of time, many will experience fatigue. This may invoke a feeling of heaviness in the arms and legs, creating the illusion that more effort is needed to perform basic movements. Autogenic training, a mental training strategy used by many elite athletes in Europe, teaches athletes to intentionally create this feeling of warmth and heaviness in the arms and legs. This training strategy uses the sensation of heaviness as a form of self-hypnosis. It teaches athletes to control their body by producing the feeling of heaviness and then counteracting that feeling with relaxing thoughts. Autogenic training is an example of how a player can use her mind to control how her body responds when fatigue has set in. Drill 31: Relay With Tired Arms is designed to produce feelings of fatigue and then strategically alter these feelings.

Energy Under Pressure

Coaches often tell their players to be quick rather than fast. A player who performs a skill fast will use hurried, rushed movements that often lead to errors. Players need to be quick without rushing or hurrying their actions. For example, when a runner is on first and a ball is hit up the middle, a second-base player will field the ball and make an underhand toss to the shortstop in an attempt to get the runner at second. In her haste to get the lead out and possibly turn the double play, the second-base player may rush her toss to the shortstop. This will increase her chances of making an inaccurate toss, which may result in only getting one out or even allowing both runners to advance safely. Another situation in which a quick underhand toss is very important is during a squeeze play. When the bunt goes down, a fielder may rush her actions out of fear that the runner will beat the throw to home plate. Unfortunately, this may force an errant toss that allows the runner to score without a challenge. To avoid this disaster, a fielder must be quick while maintaining control of her movements. Drill 32: Quick Underhand Toss gives players the opportunity to practice quick, but precise, fielding techniques.

31 *Relay With Tired Arms*

Mental Skill Energy regulation

Physical Skill Throwing

Purpose   To teach players to identify and regulate muscle fatigue or tension in the arms

Equipment   Weighted balls

Implementation   Organize players into groups of three. Each group forms a throwing line with approximately 40 feet between players. Players throw the ball in a relay format—the player in the middle receives and throws the ball to each player on the ends. The coach times this relay activity for one minute. During the first minute, the players use a weighted softball to produce the feeling of fatigue that may occur late in a game. The player in the center of the relay rapidly throws the ball to her teammates on either end; therefore, her arm should begin to feel heavy or fatigued. After throwing for one minute, the player in the center should come up with a cue word associated with a feeling of lightness or ease of throwing. Retaining the same positions, the players repeat the throwing sequence for another minute, but they use a regular softball. This will make them aware of the difference between the feeling of heaviness and lightness. During the second minute, the player in the center should silently repeat her cue word. The goal is for the player to associate this word with the feeling of lightness so that she can use it to replicate this feeling when experiencing fatigue in a game situation. Rotate positions and repeat the drill so that each player gets a chance to be in the center position.

Scoring   The player in the center of the relay counts the number of throws she completes during both one-minute sequences (with and without the weighted ball).

Coaching Tip   Encourage accuracy, quick releases, and good relay techniques throughout the drill.

32   *Quick Underhand Toss*

Mental Skill   Energy regulation

Physical Skill   Fielding, underhand toss

Purpose   To help players increase the speed and accuracy of underhand tosses in pressure situations

Implementation   Split infielders into two teams. One group forms a line midway between third and home, and the other group forms a line midway between first and home. Position a low stationary target (below the knees) at home plate. Two feeders stand on either side of the target (see figure 6.1). The feeder on the third-base side will gently roll ground balls to fielders on the first-base side, while simultaneously the feeder on the first-base side will gently roll ground balls to the third-base side (to provide realistic ball angles in a bunting situation). On cue, the feeders roll ground balls simultaneously. The first fielder in each line charges her ball and makes a bare-handed underhand toss to the target. Before fielding, each player should recite a cue word (such as "still," "stay," or "calm") to control her movements to make a quick and accurate toss.

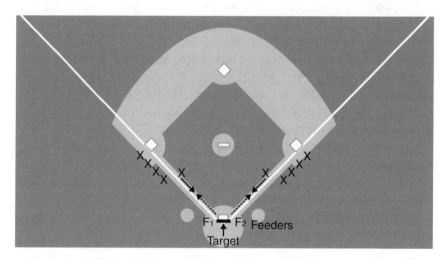

Figure 6.1   Quick Underhand Toss.

Scoring   The fielder who hits the target first receives a point for her team, and the first team to accumulate 10 points wins the drill.

Variation   The lead-up to this competition could be for middle infielders to practice at second base, while pitchers, first-, and third-base players practice it at home plate. Then combine the groups and have a competition between the two groups.

CONCENTRATION

There are many situations in which infielders may experience periods of inattentiveness. For instance, an infielder may become too relaxed and have difficulty maintaining her concentration when she is not getting much action, when she is feeling fatigued, or when her team is ahead or behind by many runs.

The major job of all infielders is to take care of the ball when they become involved in a play. To field with precision, a player must perform one task at a time (for example, fielding before throwing or catching before tagging). When fielding a ball, a common mistake players make is to track the ball until a certain point but lift their head prematurely, before the ball is completely in the glove. The likelihood of making a fielding error increases when a player takes her eyes off of the ball, especially if it is spinning hard or takes a funny hop. Drill 33: Stripes "R" Us is designed to improve a player's ability to maintain focus throughout the fielding motion. In this drill, a player must identify the number of stripes on the ball to make the correct fielding response. This forces players to keep their eyes on the ball. (Refer back to figure 4.1 on page 82 for details on creating striped balls.)

Coaches often use phrases such as "You play like you practice" or "What we do in practice will carry over into games." Although coaches emphasize the importance of playing and practicing with the same level of effort and intensity, many infield practice drills do not foster an environment that replicates the mental and physical demands encountered in games.

Most infielders are capable of making direct or indirect contributions to each play. For example, when a ball is hit during a game, a player's immediate response is a slight movement in the direction of the ball. Her subsequent response may include fielding the ball, covering a base, backing up a teammate, or communicating to help direct the play. To do this, a player must focus her attention on the ball, her teammates, the base runners, and any other information necessary to complete the play. Fortunately, most players are good at focusing on these factors because they have been trained to pay attention to relevant cues in various situations. However, the demands during games require the player to apply her attention for a longer duration than during practices.

In games, each player is affected by the consequences of her actions, but she is also affected by her teammates' actions. It is easy for a player to focus her attention on every play during competition because she knows that the outcome of each action may have an impact on her next decision and subsequent action. Unfortunately, practice drills are rarely designed to emulate this aspect of real games, where the consequences of individual actions affect the actions of others. For instance, many coaches conduct a drill in which infielders take turns fielding and throwing to bases.

Typically starting with the third-base player, each player fields one or two balls and throws to a particular base; in the meantime, other players wait for their turn. Although the primary goal of this drill is to get players warmed up before practicing more complex game situations, most players are just standing around. When a player is not physically involved in a play, she is usually not mentally involved either. Many players will use this time to relax, tune out, or talk to teammates. A player can take this mental break from the action because she knows that she will not be participating in the play. In addition, making an error or missing a ball in practice does not have a direct impact on winning a game or improving team statistics. In fact, a player who makes a fielding mistake in practice will often get a second chance to perform the same play correctly. Therefore, it may be difficult for a player to focus on the actions of her teammates because she knows they will not have an effect on her own actions. Unfortunately, the duration of a player's attention during infield practice does not mimic the duration of attention required for performance in games.

To achieve an optimal level of performance, it is important to practice both mental and physical skills in the same manner in which they are used in games. Therefore, a player must learn to focus her attention in practice with the same level of effort and intensity demanded in competition. Drill 34: 1-2-3 Stripes You're Out is designed to keep the outcome of each play unknown so that players must remain attentive during every play. This will help improve the duration of player focus, enhance communication among team members, and reduce inactivity.

Fielding With Distractions

During a game, the infielders may encounter many potential distractions. Some distractions occur within the field of play, and some occur beyond the confines of the game. These distractions may include fans who are yelling or gesturing from the stands, chants by the opposition, questionable calls by an umpire, an uneven playing surface, or poor weather conditions. If a player is distracted between pitches, she is neglecting to mentally prepare herself for the next play. For example, a player who fails to analyze the game situation before each pitch may forget the number of outs. If the ball is hit to her, she may respond with an incorrect decision such as throwing to the wrong base. If a player is distracted at the moment she is making a play on the ball, the result may not be a bad decision, but a fielding error. Regardless of when they occur, a player must learn to overcome distractions by maintaining focus on the relevant cues to successfully complete the required task. One of the most common infield distractions occurs when a base runner crosses the path of a fielder while she is making a play on the ball. For example, a second-base player who is fielding a ground ball may become distracted by a runner who is advancing from first to second base. If she focuses her attention on the runner or tries to make a play before she has complete control of the ball, she increases the chances of mishandling the ball. Drill 35: Fielding With Distractions is designed to improve the middle infielder's ability to block out distractions by focusing her attention on the ball while making a play.

Cues

A trigger word is a simple tool to direct attention when initiating an action. When fielding a bunt, players at first and third will charge the ball. One of those players is expected to field the ball and make a throw to a base. Depending on the situation, she will either make an attempt to get the lead runner or take the guaranteed out at first base. Regardless of where the out is made, the player must react

COACH'S FAVORITE DRILL

Coach Patrick Murphy has served as head softball coach at the University of Alabama for five seasons. He has led the Crimson Tide to four consecutive NCAA Division I tournaments and his team also appeared in the 2000 Women's College World Series. Coach Murphy offers his favorite infield drill to teach the proper mechanics of throwing and catching on the run.

Photo courtesy of University of Alabama Athletics

Patrick Murphy, head softball coach, University of Alabama

(continued)

Circle Catch

Mental Skill   Concentration

Physical Skills   Hand–eye coordination, catching, throwing

Purpose   To teach infielders the proper mechanics of throwing and catching on the run

Implementation   Partner infielders will with a teammate. Then, as a coach, teach the proper mechanics of a "dart throw" prior to implementing this drill. A dart throw is a short toss used mainly by infielders during a close play at one of the bases. The infielder should have the ball in her hand, which is cocked in an upside-down L position. She then tosses the ball overhand using mainly her wrist for momentum. It is not a full throw as most "dart throws" are at close distances. The coach then has the infielders stand next to each other about 10 feet apart. The infielders will shuffle in a circle while executing the "dart throw" to each other. After 15 seconds, the coach will say, "other way" and the infielders will shuffle in the opposite direction.

Coaching Tips

- This is a very advanced drill and may take several times before proper execution.
- When the athletes can execute the drill, increase the time playing circle catch.

and throw as quickly and efficiently as possible. This sometimes involves pivoting the body and making a throw in the same movement. Therefore, a player must make a decision while shifting her attention as quickly as possible from fielding the ball to making a throw. Drill 36: Fielding the Bunt emphasizes reaction time, cue recognition, and accuracy while fielding a bunt.

33   *Stripes "R" Us*

Mental Skill   Concentration

Physical Skill   Fielding and throwing

Purpose   To improve players' reaction time and decision making while fielding ground balls and throwing for accuracy

Implementation (See figure 6.2)   Position three targets (one stripe, two stripes, and three stripes) at chest level on a hitting screen or fence. The coach is positioned to the right side of the targets with a bucket of striped balls that correspond to the three targets. Position the infielders approximately 60 feet from the coach in a single-file line. The distance should be similar to the distance from home plate to the players' respective positions, so corner infielders may be positioned closer to the coach and middle infielders positioned farther away. Each player will field two balls before rotating. When a ball is hit by the coach, the fielder must recognize the number of stripes, field the ball, and throw to the corresponding target.

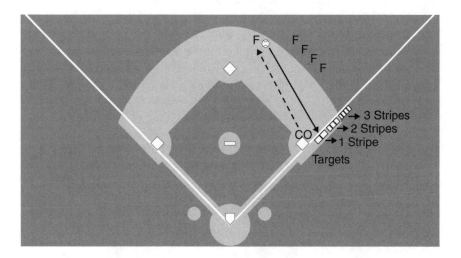

Figure 6.2   Stripes "R" Us.

Scoring   Record the number of successful throws to the correct target.

Coaching Tip   Before each hit, the coach must hold the ball so that the infielder cannot detect the ball markings (number of stripes) before the ball is contacted.

Variation   To decrease the difficulty, conduct the drill using two instead of three targets (one with stripes and one without stripes). The coach hits balls that are either striped or not striped, and the players respond by throwing to the corresponding target.

34 1-2-3 Stripes You're Out

Mental Skill Concentration

Physical Skill Fielding and throwing

Purpose To improve players' concentration, reaction time, and communication skills while performing basic infield plays

Equipment Striped balls

Implementation Each infielder plays her primary position. The coach hits from home plate, randomly hitting ground balls to infielders. The balls are marked with stripes that correspond to a specific base. If the ball has one stripe, the play will be made at first base (two stripes = second base, three stripes = third base, no stripes = home). When a ball is hit, the fielding player must recognize the number of stripes and throw the ball to the corresponding base. Although the play will only be made at one base, each infielder must prepare to make a play at a base by reacting to the placement of each grounder and covering the appropriate base. Without knowing the number of stripes on each ball, all infielders must focus their attention on the ball and react as if they are in the play.

COACH'S FAVORITE DRILL

Photo courtesy of Tami Brown

Tami Brown, former Division I coach and director of All-American Softball School

Coach Tami Brown, former Division I coach and player, is currently the co-owner and director of the All-American Softball School's college prep program in Sacramento, California. Rapid Fire is her favorite infield drill. This drill improves cardiovascular fitness and concentration by requiring each infielder to play an active role throughout the entire duration of the drill. To execute the drill successfully, players must sustain focus for a specified number of repetitions.

Rapid Fire

Mental Skill   Concentration

Physical Skill   Fielding and throwing

Purpose   To improve cardiovascular fitness and enhance the duration of player concentration while performing in various situations on the infield

Implementation   Infielders assume their primary position. One coach (C1) hits grounders to the infielders from the left side of home plate, and another coach (C2) hits grounders to the infielders from the right side. Each coach will have a feeder/catcher. This drill includes six variations of infield plays. Rotate to the next variation after each player has fielded 15 to 20 balls.

- **Variation 1:** One coach (C1) hits grounders to the second-base player, who fields and throws to first base; the first-base player then returns the ball to the feeder (F1). The other coach (C2) hits grounders to the shortstop, who fields and throws to third base; the third-base player returns the ball to the feeder (F2). See figure 6.3 for Variation 1.

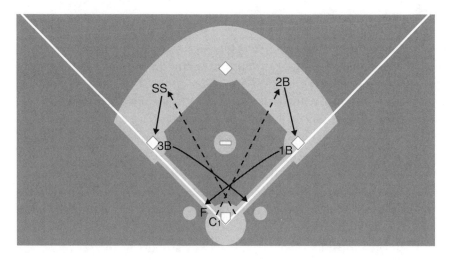

Figure 6.3   Variation 1.

(continued)

- **Variation 2:** One coach (C1) hits grounders to the second-base player, who fields and throws to the shortstop at second base; the shortstop returns the ball to the feeder (F1). The other coach (C2) hits grounders to the third-base player, who fields and throws to first base; the first-base player returns the ball to the feeder (F2). See figure 6.4 for Variation 2.

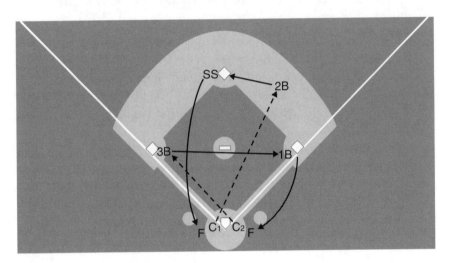

Figure 6.4   Variation 2.

- **Variation 3:** One coach (C1) hits grounders to the first-base player, who fields and throws to third base; the third-base player returns the ball to the feeder (F1). The other coach (C2) hits grounders to the shortstop, who fields and throws to second base; the second-base player returns the ball to the feeder (F2).

- **Variation 4:** One coach (C1) hits grounders to the first-base player, who fields and throws to the second-base player at first base; the first-base player returns the ball to the feeder (F1). The other coach (C2) hits grounders to the third-base player, who fields and throws to the shortstop at third base; the shortstop returns the ball to the feeder (F2).

- **Variation 5:** One coach (C1) hits grounders to the second-base player, who fields and throws to third base; the third-base player returns the ball to the feeder (F1). The other coach (C2) hits grounders to the shortstop, who fields and throws to first base; the first-base player returns the ball to the feeder (F2).

- **Variation 6:** One coach (C1) hits grounders to the first-base player, who fields and throws to the shortstop at second base; the shortstop returns the ball to the feeder (F1). The other coach (C2) hits grounders to the third-base player, who fields and throws to the second-base player at second base; the second-base player returns the ball to the feeder (F2).

Coaching Tip   The coaches should alternate hitting grounders so that players are not vulnerable to injury.

35   *Fielding With Distractions*

Mental Skill   Concentration

Physical Skill   Fielding

Purpose   To improve the middle infielders' ability to track the ball and field it while runners are in motion (potentially crossing the fielding path)

Implementation   Position a line of base runners at first and second base. The coach alternates hitting ground balls to the shortstop and second-base player. A base runner will advance when the ball is contacted. When a ball is hit to the shortstop, the runner on second advances to third base; when a ball is hit to the second-base player, the runner on first advances to second base. Just before contact, the infielder should use a cue word (such as ball, down, attack) to focus attention on fielding the ball. The fielder plays the ball while the runner is approaching the fielding path. The fielder completes the play by throwing to first base or another base designated by the coach. (Position a receiver at the base where the play is being made.)

36   *Fielding the Bunt*

Mental Skill   Concentration

Physical Skill   Fielding a bunt

Purpose   To improve the corner infielders' reaction time when fielding and throwing to a base in a bunt situation

Implementation Instruct the first- and third-base players to each draw their own line in the dirt midway between first base and home plate, and third base and home plate. Starting from behind the line, players will alternate fielding five bunts each. The coach uses balls that are marked with one, two, or three stripes. When fielding the bunt, the fielder must recognize the number of stripes on the ball and throw to the base that corresponds with this number (one stripe = first base, two stripes = second base, three stripes = third base, no stripes = home plate). The fielder should call out the number of stripes on each ball immediately after she recognizes the correct number to help initiate her response. Position extra infielders at each base to receive throws. After throwing to the appropriate base, the player quickly returns to her starting line to prepare for the next play. Repeat the drill for three to four cycles.

CONFIDENCE

At one time or another, an infielder may lack confidence in a certain aspect of her game. A lack of confidence is typically the result of fear—fear of failure, fear of making a mistake, fear of disappointing a coach. When a player experiences even the slightest bit of doubt, she hopes the ball will not be hit to her. Readiness, however, comes when a player expects the ball to be hit her way. This expectation can override fear or doubt by giving the player something concrete to replace her fears. Ironically, there appears to be a correlation between self-doubt and ball direction—the more a player wants to avoid being in the play, the more likely the ball will be hit in her direction. Although this magnetic field is not scientifically validated, it does appear to exist in the sport of softball. Players should be taught to want and expect the ball, every play.

Affirmations

A player's mind is often her toughest opponent. When a player doesn't know what to expect, she typically will expect the worst. She will focus on the question rather than the answer (questions such as "What if I make a mistake?" or "What if the ball is hit to me?"). In general, people ask questions when they are unsure of the answer or outcome. A question is a representation of doubt, because if they knew the answer they would have no reason to question. Coaches should teach players to focus on the answer (such as "If I make a mistake, I need to learn from it and be resilient" or "When the ball is hit to me, I'm throwing to first"). A player can choose to focus on the question, which implies doubt, or the answer, which implies confidence. Fortunately, a player is capable of controlling her mind and can use strategies to avoid giving her mind an opportunity to doubt. Following is a simple game that teaches players to trust in their ability. To enact this trust, drill 37: React and Release is designed so players must quickly respond to a stimulus without having time to think. This will help them regain or build their confidence in their instinctive athletic ability.

Trusting in Ability Exercise

Most of the time, when a player must react without thinking, she will be successful. A coach can demonstrate this by tossing a softball to a player who is not looking. Call her name to let her know it is coming, but don't give her much time to react. Her likely response will be to recognize the ball in midair and make a good catch. She can do this because she has the natural athletic ability that allows her to simply react. But when she has time to think, these natural responses may decrease, especially if her thoughts are negative or filled with doubt.

This simple reaction response can be translated into real situations, such as throwing the ball to a base. To practice this, designate three targets along a fence. Position the player about 20 to 30 feet from the fence. Continuously throw or roll softballs to the player. Instruct her to just get the ball and throw to a target. Do not give her time to reset in between throws because this will give her time to think. The goal is for the player to react without thinking in order to regain belief in her natural athletic ability and affirm trust in her instincts. Do a sequence of about 10 balls. Let the player take a break, then repeat.

Positive Self-Talk

When refining a skill, or when performance is suffering, it is easy for players to make errors and become frustrated. Consequently, a player will become doubtful and begin questioning her ability. This often leads to negative thinking, which influences subsequent actions. Drill 38: Bumped Out teaches players to use mental strategies to process errors and reaffirm confidence in fielding. This drill

Telling yourself you can make the play is the first step in good defense.

also reinforces the ability to be resilient in the face of mistakes. The mind is what controls how the body responds when performing a skill. If a player is thinking negatively, these thoughts will contribute to her inability to perform. Refer to figure 6.5 for an exercise that demonstrates how thoughts have the capacity to influence actions.

When players complete plays, they should do so with authority. Coaches must help players develop a confident fielding attitude to be more aggressive and less timid. Playing aggressively allows the player to attack the ball, whereas playing timidly allows the ball to control the player. For example, if a high chopper is hit to a fielder, she must take away the hop by charging the ball. If she plays timidly and waits for the ball to get to her, the ball will take more bounces, increasing the chances that it will take a bad hop. Waiting on the ball also gives the base runner more time to safely get to first base. If the fielder uses a word or phrase to help direct her attention toward charging the ball, she will be more likely to make an aggressive play on the ball. This aggressive attitude can be taught using methods from drill 39: Fielding With Authority.

Communication

Effective communication is important for building confidence and trust among teammates. In between pitches, infielders should com-

Figure 6.5   The Power of Thought

Many players underestimate the power of their thoughts. When we are thinking, we are conducting an internal dialogue with ourselves. There is evidence suggesting that people engage in internal dialogues, which amount to 150 to 300 words per minute totaling 45,000 to 51,000 thoughts per day. Our internal dialogue sends signals to our body, which influence how we act and behave. If we think positively, our mind will send positive signals to the body and if we think negatively, our mind will send negative signals to our body. To demonstrate to an athlete the extent to which her thoughts influence her actions, perform this simple exercise.

- Instruct the athlete to fully extend her throwing arm out in front of her body.
- With her arm extended, tell her to close her eyes.
- While her eyes are closed, provide this or a similar scenario to convey to her that her arm is very fatigued and heavy.
- You have been throwing all day… Your arm feels sore and heavy… You feel like you are holding a 20-pound brick…and you can barely hold it up any longer… Your arm is so tired that you want to let it fall to your side, but you can't.
- After about 30 seconds of negative statements, instruct the athlete to provide resistance while you apply downward pressure on her hand.
- Allow her to rest her arm for 30 seconds.
- Repeat the drill, but this time after the athlete closes her eyes and extends her arm, provide only positive statements about how strong her arm feels.
- You feel so strong right now… Your arm is like a steel wall that nothing can penetrate… You feel like you can lift anything… You can stop anything… You are stronger than you've ever been.
- Once again, after 30 seconds, instruct the athlete to provide resistance while you apply downward pressure on her hand.
- You and the athlete will notice that she is able to resist more pressure and she will feel stronger after listening to the positive versus the negative statement.
- For this reason, when performing any type of softball skill, it is important that athletes think positive thoughts.

municate with one another to set up plays, anticipate actions, and relay messages to the outfield. As a play develops, players on a good defensive unit will help direct each other to reinforce the necessary responses for efficient playmaking. A player must have a good idea of what her teammates are thinking so that she is not surprised if a ball is suddenly thrown in her direction.

Communication is also important between two players who are responsible for covering the same base. For example, when a runner is on first base and a ball is hit up the middle, the shortstop and second-base player must decide who will field the ball and who will cover the base. Inadequate communication on this play, which is ideally a double play situation, could result in a collision between these players (likely allowing both runners to advance safely). Therefore, effective communication is highly important, and it is the obligation of each player to take responsibility for conveying messages to teammates. Not only should the infield communicate with each other, but they are also responsible for communicating and relaying messages to the outfield. Drill 40: Who's Got It? will help players develop a sense of trust in their ability to communicate with each other, and this will carry over into other aspects of infield defense.

37 React and Release

Mental Skill   Confidence

Physical Skill   Fielding and throwing

Purpose   To improve players' confidence in their ability to field ground balls and make accurate throws to specified targets

Implementation   Form two lines of infielders behind one of the base paths, one line for corner players and one line for middle infielders. The distance used for this drill should be similar to the distance from home plate to the players' respective positions, so corner infielders may be positioned closer to the targets and middle infielders positioned farther away. The coach positions three targets (striped) along a fence or screen. Players rotate fielding one ground ball at a time. Just before the player fields the ball, the coach calls out a number that corresponds to the number of stripes on one of the three targets (one, two, or three). The player must field the ball and respond to the call by throwing to hit the correct target.

38 Bumped Out

Mental Skill   Confidence

Physical Skill   Fielding

Purpose   To practice positive affirmations and improve players' confidence after experiencing failure

Implementation Designate one player for each defensive position (both infield and outfield). The coach sets up various game situations and randomly hits to fielders. If a fielder makes an error, she is automatically bumped from the game. A replacement player immediately fills her position. Outfielders will replace outfielders and infielders will replace infielders (although it may not be their primary position). When a player is tossed from the scrimmage, the player should evaluate the error and determine what she could have done differently. This evaluation should be followed up with positive self-talk to reinforce the belief that she is a good defensive player. Players who are not in a defensive position will serve as base runners.

39 Fielding With Authority

Mental Skill Confidence

Physical Skill Fielding

Purpose To help players build confidence by playing aggressively and by demonstrating confidence through physical actions

Implementation During infield practice, conduct a controlled scrimmage and instruct players to complete plays with authority. When making a play, each fielder should display a competitive, serious, and confident demeanor. Players must exude confidence through body language; this should include good posture, a solid ready position, eyes alert, and good anticipation. Don't allow players to drag feet or hunch shoulders. Encourage players to develop a "love to field, ready to field, going to make a play" attitude.

40 Who's Got It?

Mental Skill Confidence

Physical Skill Infield defense

Purpose To improve players' communication skills and develop trust between teammates and confidence that the play will be made in a pop-up situation

Implementation (see figure 6.6) Form two lines of infielders approximately 15 feet apart. The coach is positioned about 40 feet in front of the two lines. The first player in each line lies down on her stomach facing away from the coach. The coach throws a fly ball between the

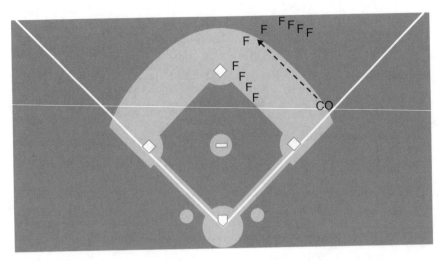

Figure 6.6 Who's Got It?

two players who are lying down. On the release, the coach yells, "Go!" The players respond to this command by getting on their feet, locating the ball, communicating about who will make the catch, and completing the play.

Scoring   As a team, keep track of the number of successful catches out of the total number of attempts.

MENTAL IMAGERY

Errors are a part of the game. Sometimes they are mental and sometimes they are physical, but inevitably they are going to occur. Even when a defensive player is thoroughly prepared and completely in tune with every play, physical errors will occasionally happen because no one is perfect. Coaches commonly tell their players that physical mistakes are part of the game and it is the mental mistakes that are not acceptable. This sounds logical, but since all players seek performance excellence, they will experience frustration after making a mistake whether it is physical or mental. The most deadly mistake a defensive player can make is the combination of a physical error followed by a mental error. For example, if a ground ball is hit to the shortstop, and she bobbles the ball while preparing to make the play at first base, she should respond by holding the ball. Unfortunately, a player in this situation may become anxious and force a throw without having full control of the ball. This may cause an overthrow, which will not only allow the runner to safely reach first, but also allow her to advance one or two extra bases. Through the use of mental imagery, players have the ability to correct each play and therefore the ability to play perfect softball. The following two drills, drill 41: Make a Play—Fake a Play and drill 42: In It to Win It, provide opportunities to use mental imagery to improve fielding performance.

41 *Make a Play—Fake a Play*

Mental Skill Mental imagery

Physical Skill Fielding and throwing

Purpose To improve players' ability to consistently perform proper mechanics and quickly recover from errors by mentally rehearsing perfect fielding

Implementation Infielders assume their primary defensive position. The coach hits ground balls from home plate, alternating ground balls to each player. Simulate various defensive situations, or practice skills such as fielding ground balls and throwing to bases, turning double plays, or fielding bunts. Base runners are optional. Regardless of outcome, after each play is complete, the primary fielder should imagine a perfect execution of the same play. She should then physically simulate making the play with precise fielding technique from beginning to end. Keep up the pace by hitting to other positions while fielders are engaging in mental and physical re-creations.

42 *In It to Win It*

Mental Skill Mental imagery

Physical Skill Fielding

Purpose To allow players to practice fielding ground balls on the infield while using mental imagery to recall successful plays and correct unsuccessful plays

Implementation (see figure 6.7) Form two lines of infielders behind one of the base paths, one line for corner players and one line for middle infielders. The distance used for this drill should be similar to the distance from home plate to the players' respective positions, so corner infielders may be positioned closer to the targets and middle infielders positioned

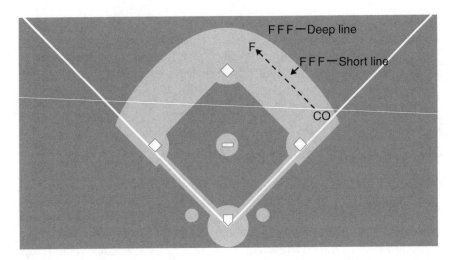

Figure 6.7 In It to Win It.

farther away. The coach will hit 10 rounds of ground balls to the entire team. Players will rotate after fielding one ball; a round is complete when each fielder has received one ground ball. After properly fielding a ball, the player should imagine herself successfully fielding the exact same play. If a player misses or bobbles a grounder, the player should imagine herself correcting the error and performing the same play correctly.

Scoring Each player counts the number of successful plays out of 10.

Coaching Tips

- Increase the difficulty of grounders in later rounds of competition.
- Players can compete to reach personal goals or against teammates.
- Players should create a goal before participating in the competition (for example, increasing the number of successful plays).

MENTAPHYSICAL WRAP-UP

For every pitch of every inning of every game (typically between 70 to 90 pitches per game), the defense must be aware of the playing conditions and the immediate game situation, including the inning, the number of outs, runners on base, and the count. Each time a pitch is thrown, there is potential for a change in plan for each defensive player. Players must be alert and attentive on every play, but with a game tempo that often facilitates lulls in the action, this can be difficult. An infielder may not be as sharp if she has not received a ball for the entire game or if the pitcher takes a long time in between pitches. To prepare players for each pitch, a pre-performance routine is essential. Drill 43: Prepare for the Play enables the infielders to practice their defensive pre-performance routines. This routine should be used before each play in practice and in competition.

43 *Prepare for the Play*

Mental Skill   Energy regulation, concentration, confidence, mental imagery

Physical Skill   Infield defense

Purpose   To help fielders develop a pre-performance routine to be used before the delivery of each pitch

Implementation   Conduct a controlled scrimmage. The pitcher will simulate the pitching motion. The coach hits ground balls and sets up various defensive situations for the infield. After each play is complete, all fielders should perform a pre-performance routine. An infielder's pre-performance routine may include the following elements:

- Relay the number of outs
- Scan the field in preparation for the next play
- Get into fielding ready position, directing focus to the catcher
- Relay the signs to the outfield
- Focus on the pitch

7

Outfield Defense

Players in the outfield serve as an extension of the infield. Young players may find playing the outfield boring and may feel uninvolved or removed from the pitch-by-pitch action that occurs on the infield. More experienced players, on the other hand, realize the importance of the outfield and take pride in their unique role as the last line of defense. The contributions of outfielders are vitally important for team success as each outfielder tries to prevent the ball from getting past her. If a ball gets by an outfielder, it is almost certain that base runners will advance one or two bases. Although it may seem uneventful at times, playing an outfield position is certainly a challenge for any player.

The primary role of outfielders is to provide backup to the infielders for hard hit grounders, overthrows, pop-ups, pick-offs, and steals. They chase after balls that are hit with extreme power and field the hits that travel through gaps in the infield. Although the outfield positions are extremely important, the number of opportunities to make plays is limited, especially if the pitcher is throwing a good game. Therefore, it is critical that outfielders stay fully prepared when their services are needed. For every pitch, each outfielder must reposition herself depending on a variety of factors, including the batter's stance and hitting tendencies, the count, the number of outs, the score, the inning, and any other factors that are pertinent to the immediate game situation. For example, imagine that a game is tied in the bottom of the seventh inning. There are less than two outs, and the opposing team has a runner on third base. In this situation, a left fielder should know that the most effective positioning is in mid to shallow left field. If she is playing too deep, a sacrifice fly will easily score the run from third base.

Every time a pitch is delivered, an outfielder should make an initial movement in the direction that the ball is likely to travel. If she is not directly involved in the play, she will adjust and attend to any backup responsibilities. Great outfielders possess acute depth perception. When a ball is hit from home plate, it is approximately 180 to 200 feet from the outfield positions. Tracking a relatively small object that is traveling at speeds of up to 100 miles per hour requires astute visual and temporal judgments.

Playing an outfield position is quite different from playing an infield position. First, outfielders have more time to react. Second, the response to a play is not always as predictable in the outfield as it is in the infield. For example, when the ball is hit to an infielder, the correct play is usually obvious. But when the ball is hit to an outfielder, the correct response may not be as easy to decipher, especially if runners are advancing to different bases at the same time. Third, not only do the infielders know where the play will be made, but they also get numerous opportunities to make the right play. Depending on the position, infielders are typically directly involved in 10 to 20 plays a game. Outfielders, on the other hand, may only get 3 or 4 chances to make a play. Therefore, they must be fully ready when this opportunity comes. If a player prepares herself correctly, she can avoid the downward performance spiral that accompanies mistakes during competition. Fourth, while infielders have the luxury of knowing they have backup support, outfielders do not enjoy this comfort. Outfielders provide the backup and position themselves strategically in order to cover overthrows or fluke situations. If a ball gets by an outfielder, this spells trouble. Fifth, unlike infielders, who are positioned a few yards apart, outfielders have a lot of distance between each other. Thus, developing effective modes of communication between outfielders is critical.

In the two hours it takes to complete a softball game, playing an outfield position allows ample time to think. If players use this time to think negatively, it could affect the outcome of the game. Outfielders are often up against brutal, and uncontrollable, playing conditions. They are more likely than infielders to be impacted by the sun, wind, uneven turf, and wet conditions. These conditions make it difficult to throw the ball with both force and accuracy. Sometimes an outfielder is lucky if she even gets to make a play on one ball during an entire seven-inning game. If an outfielder only gets one chance to do her job during a game, and fails, she will not feel good about her performance. Therefore, when the opportunity to make a play does occur, it is vitally important that each outfielder is properly prepared to respond.

ENERGY REGULATION

During the course of a softball game, outfielders must be able to increase, decrease, and conserve their energy depending on the demands of the game. Playing in the outfield often involves standing and waiting for long periods of time. Inning after inning, this can be physically draining and mentally understimulating. For some outfielders, this lack of movement may cause muscular stiffness and unwanted muscle tension. By the time they get an opportunity to make a play on the ball, their muscles are no longer loose. Tense muscles do not allow for optimally coordinated movements that are required for successful fielding. Muscle tension increases the chance of making an error. In contrast, other outfielders may experience the opposite effect. They may become too relaxed and may be unable to respond to a play with authority. Therefore, outfielders must be able to get their energy up or to bring it down on command. For a player to manage her energy level, the key is to identify it and adapt it according to the demands of the situation.

Managing Energy Level

Outfielders should learn to expend and ration energy so that they are at an optimal level when their services are needed. Drill 44: Sprint and Sit will allow players to practice ways of identifying and monitoring energy according to the requirements of a task.

Although outfielders experience a lot of downtime, when they do get a chance to contribute, the plays are typically exciting and require an extraordinary amount of energy. The plays often involve an attempt to throw a runner out at one of the bases or home plate. If an outfielder is making a play on a ball in front of her, she can see what is happening on the field. If she knows the play is going to be close, this may cause her to panic or to rush her actions, and she may try to throw the runner out before completely gaining control of her body and the ball. This is an example of an intensity level that has exceeded the necessary level for optimal performance. When players get into pressure situations, they will often sacrifice correct technique in an attempt to make a play. Drill 45: One Step Ahead addresses this tendency by emphasizing calm and controlled movements under pressure.

44 *Sprint and Sit*

Mental Skill   Energy regulation

Physical Skill   Outfield defense

Purpose   To help players identify sources of tension when transitioning between high and low intensity levels

Implementation   Create two stations in the outfield.

- *Station one: high intensity.* The fielder is positioned in the center of six cones placed in a circular formation in the outfield (30 to 40 feet apart). Fly balls will be thrown near the center of the circle. The fielder catches a ball, then sprints to any one of the cones, drops the ball off, and returns to the center to catch the next ball. Repeat until a ball is placed at each cone.

* *Station two: low intensity.* The player lies down, closes her eyes, and takes three deep breaths. She identifies areas of the body where she is experiencing tension. The player then creates additional tension in that area by flexing the muscles, holding for five seconds, then releasing the tension. Repeat the tension and relaxation sequence three times for each targeted area.

Rotate players between stations every three to five minutes.

Scoring   Keep track of the amount of time it takes to place balls on all six cones.

Coaching Tip   Be sure that the players are expending 100 percent of their energy while at the high-intensity station and deliberate relaxation (not just laying down to rest) while at the low-intensity station.

Variation   Any type of high-intensity drill designed to work on outfield skills can be used at station one. Other relaxation strategies or mental imagery exercises can be integrated into station two.

45   *One Step Ahead*

Mental Skill   Energy regulation

Physical Skill   Outfield defense

Purpose   To help players improve fielding speed and accuracy in pressure situations by practicing calm and controlled movements

Implementation   Position a line of base runners at first base. Outfielders assume their primary positions. The coach hits from home plate to any of the outfield positions. When the ball is contacted, a base runner will advance from first to second. The goal of the outfielder is to cleanly field the ball and make a quick and accurate throw to second base to beat the runner. Between each play, outfielders should scan the field and prepare for the next play by saying a cue word (such as "react" or "pace") that helps them to be ready and to avoid rushing their performance. Repeat the drill several times hitting to various field locations. Continue the drill with runners beginning on second base. The goal of the outfielders is to make a quick and accurate throw to third base to beat the runner.

Scoring Each outfielder keeps track of the number of successful throws out of the total number of opportunities.

Variation To increase the difficulty, runners may advance two bases (for example, from first to third or from second to home).

CONCENTRATION

A great outfielder can often predict the direction that a ball will be hit before it connects with the bat. Although this is not a rare skill, it does take practice and mental discipline. In order to make this prediction, an outfielder must use a broad external attention style before each pitch. Her attention should be directed to the immediate game situation—the count, the number of outs, the hitter's stance in the batter's box, the type of pitch being thrown, and the location of the pitch. Once the ball is contacted, the outfielder must immediately shift her attention to a new set of cues (still broad external) in order to make a play on the ball or to respond appropriately in a backup capacity. At this point, she will pay attention to the angle at which the ball is contacted, the height and speed of trajectory, and the location where she must position herself to make a catch or to cut the ball off and make a play. While this sequence of events may seem complicated, it becomes even more challenging when considering the situational and environmental factors an outfielder may encounter.

One situation that is a challenge in the outfield is when runners are on base and a hitter blasts a fly ball or line drive past one of the outfielders. This is one of the few instances in which a player is forced to turn her back on the field. The player must focus her attention on the ball, using a narrow external attention style, but she must also demonstrate a broad external awareness of the game situation. She may have an idea of where the runners are and of what is happening on the field, but she must rely on her teammates to relay information about exactly where the ball should be thrown once she is able to retrieve it. The excitement generated in this type of situation and the elevated noise of the crowd make it even more difficult. Players will often report, "I couldn't hear anybody, so I just threw the ball to the first person I saw." Therefore, each outfielder must develop an acute auditory sense. Although outfielders must get the ball to an infielder as soon as possible, if the ball is thrown to the wrong player, this could cause confusion or allow a runner to advance. When a player cannot see the situation, her ability to trust her auditory sense becomes very important. The difficult part of drill 46: Ears the Play is trying to focus on auditory cues while quickly getting to the ball.

Overcoming the Elements

There are a lot of uncontrollable elements in the outfield compared to other defensive positions. Because of this, players must exercise both physical and mental flexibility. Along with situational challenges, outfielders are often confronted with adverse environmental conditions. When facing these conditions, outfielders must have great discipline in order to maintain an intense level of concentration. The sun is an element that will inevitably confront all outfielders at some time or another. When a fly ball is lost in the sun, many players will shy away in fear of being hit. Drill 47: Sun Ball is designed to improve player concentration and improve the ability to track the ball as it travels through the sun by providing a safe learning environment.

46 *Ears the Play*

Mental Skill Concentration

Physical Skill Outfield defense

Purpose To teach players to run down deep fly balls (over the fielder's head) and respond to a verbal signal

Equipment Striped balls

Implementation The coach positions three targets (one stripe, two stripes, and three stripes—see figure 7.1) along a fence or a screen. The outfielders form a line in the outfield. The coach throws or hits a fly ball over the head of the first fielder in line. While one outfielder is fielding the ball, the next player in line calls out a number (one, two, or three) that corresponds to one of the striped targets. Once the outfielder hears the signal, she calls out the number to gear her attention toward the correct target (this will also demonstrate to the coach that she heard the correct signal). The fielder completes the play by throwing the ball at the designated target.

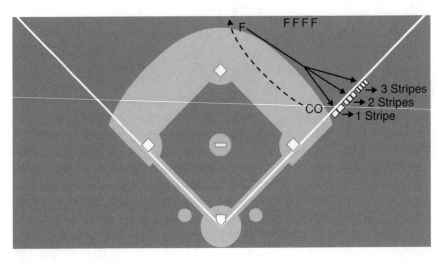

Figure 7.1 Ears the Play.

47 *Sun Ball*

Mental Skill   Concentration

Physical Skill   Outfield defense

Purpose   To help players stay focused and trust in their ability to track and catch a fly ball hit directly into the sun

Equipment   Foam softballs

Implementation   Players need a partner for this drill. One partner (the fielder) is facing the sun, and the other partner (the feeder) has her back to the sun. The feeder tosses high fly balls (foam softballs) directly into the sun. The fielder tracks the ball through the sun, attempting to make a clean catch. While tracking the ball through the sun, the fielder should repeat a self-talk phrase (such as "stay with it" or "keep tracking") that will help her maintain concentration on the ball without giving up in this difficult situation. After 10 successful catches, partners switch positions and repeat the drill.

Variation   To increase the difficulty of this drill, line up the fielders in the outfield and hit balls into the sun from a greater distance; continue using foam softballs until fielders gain confidence through successful performances.

Photo courtesy of Bob Solorio

Kathy Strahan, head coach, California State University, Sacramento

Coach Kathy Strahan has been at the helm of Sacramento State softball for 11 years. Windy City Balls is her favorite drill for developing team communication skills. Communication is a key ingredient for defensive play. One factor that challenges communication and concentration is playing in windy conditions. The wind creates a situation where players must continually shift and adjust to the unpredictable flight of the ball.

Windy City Balls

Mental Skill   Concentration

Physical Skill   Outfield defense

Purpose   To develop players' ability to concentrate and communicate in a changing environment

Implementation (see figure 7.2)   Create a square formation with four lines of outfielders on the grass. The distance between the short fielders and long fielders should represent the distance between infielders and outfielders on a regular playing field. The width between fielders should represent the width between two outfielders. The coach hits fly balls between all fielders from approximately 100 feet. The first player in each line attempts to make the play. The players must assess the wind conditions and communicate with each other to determine who is in the best position to make the catch or field the ball. Players must focus attention on the ball while communicating with teammates. After each play, fielders rotate to the next line in a clockwise direction.

Coaching Tip   Because this drill fosters team communication, it can also be used on calmer days when the wind is not a factor. Players in

(continued)

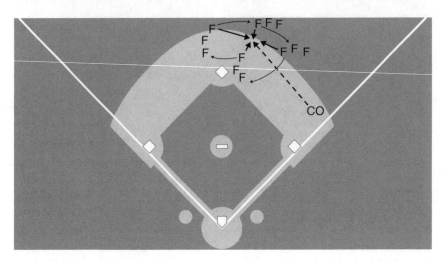

Figure 7.2 Windy City Balls.

the lines farthest from the coach will act as the outfielders and therefore have priority over calling the ball. Once a player calls for the ball, all other players (even those waiting in line) should confirm the play by calling that player's name.

CONFIDENCE

When a ball is hit to the outfield and a runner is attempting to score, an outfielder must change her mind-set and adopt a do-or-die type of attitude. Instead of playing it safe by dropping down on one knee (to ensure that she keeps the ball in front of her), the urgency on this type of play requires the fielder to play the ball off her nondominant foot while continuing to charge forward. Keeping her momentum in the direction of the play will allow her to quickly pull up and make a more efficient throw to the plate. A player must understand that taking this risk is a win–win situation. If she takes the risk and misses, the run will score, but if she plays the ball safely, the run will score anyway. So at least by taking the risk, she puts herself in a position to make a play and increases her chances of stopping the score (possibly affecting the outcome of the game).

Overcoming Obstacles

Poor field conditions can have a negative impact on player confidence. Unfortunately, most softball diamonds are not groomed in the same manner as professional baseball stadiums. On many softball fields, the playing surface is uneven, the outfield has potholes, sprinkler heads are exposed, and the grass is not freshly mowed. If a player begins to worry about how these types of conditions might affect her performance, she may lose control over her mental and physical capabilities. For example, a fielder will not be able to control whether a ball is wet, but she can control how she handles the wet ball to assure the best grip for throwing accuracy. Because playing on a wet outfield surface is common, drill 48: Get a Grip should be used to practice under this type of condition. This drill will help players gain confidence in their ability to handle this challenge. Outfielders may also encounter a variety of other circumstances that can affect their play. See below for an exercise in disaster training.

Disaster Training

Situations will arise in softball that may cause athletes to get distracted and potentially lose confidence. Because of this the team may benefit from disaster training. Identify these possible occurrences, then practice and discuss the most effective response with athletes. Examples of these situations include poor field conditions; weather-related difficulties such as wind, rain, and sun; poor officiating; verbal taunting; and equipment failures.

Performance Accomplishments

One of the most exciting plays in softball is when an outfielder runs full speed toward a fly ball, leaves her feet, stretches her body horizontally, and reaches out to make a spectacular catch. It's an awesome feeling, not only for the player who made the catch, but also for everyone lucky enough to witness it. Unfortunately, this does not come naturally or easily to all players. Some outfielders may be timid and have a mental block when it comes to diving for a ball. Diving is a reaction that should come automatically in response to a play. If a player thinks about diving, chances are, she will stay on her feet and avoid this risky task or land awkwardly increasing the likelihood of an injury. When a skill does not come naturally, players may experience a mental block. A player may say, "I want to dive, but I don't know how," or "When I go to dive, I just can't get my body to do it." When a player is not confident or is unsure of her ability to perform a skill, her mind becomes the barrier that inhibits her from performing the skill. Once a player experiences success, even just one time, she has evidence to prove to herself that she does have the ability and fear is reduced. When learning a skill, the first try is always the most difficult. Getting over the initial fear allows a player to move on to the next level. For diving, or any other new skill, trigger words can be useful for initiating the action. Once a player knows she can dive without fear of getting hurt, she will be able to perform a diving catch automatically without hesitation. Drill 49: Do or Dive will help players build confidence in their ability to dive by experiencing success in practice. This drill is designed to work in a progression, gradually increasing in difficulty. Not only will players gain confidence in their ability to dive, but they will also have fun in the process.

48 Get a Grip

Mental Skill Confidence

Physical Skill Outfield defense

Purpose To improve players' confidence in their throwing accuracy under extreme conditions

Implementation Outfielders assume their primary positions. While conducting a common outfield drill, such as throwing to bases, the coach dips the balls into a bucket of water before hitting to the fielders.

Coaching Tips
- Remind outfielders to keep a loose grip on the ball.
- Infielders can practice footwork and glove position when applying the tag.
- This drill is good if you know wet conditions might affect an upcoming game or if the game begins early in the morning and the grass will be wet.

49 *Do or Dive*

Mental Skill   Confidence

Physical Skill   Outfield defense

Purpose   To develop players' confidence in their ability to dive for a ball (through performance success and trigger words)

Implementation   Players need a partner for this drill. The players line up on the grass with approximately 5 feet between partners. One partner is kneeling and the other is standing. The player who is standing tosses her partner 10 balls from side to side; the tosser tries to mix it up so that her partner is kept alert. Each toss should be far enough away so that the player who is kneeling must lunge for the ball. Rotate after 10 catches. Players should use a trigger word, such as "dive" or "jump," to help initiate each dive. Once both players get accustomed to the drill, increase the distance between partners to approximately 10 feet; the diver then starts from a low (crouched) fielding position instead of kneeling. Rotate after 10 catches. As players gain competence, increase the distance to approximately 20 feet and instruct the tosser to throw the ball far enough so that the diver must move her feet and dive in order to catch the ball. The final phase of this drill is for the players to line up in the outfield and practice diving for balls that are hit from a greater distance.

Scoring   Turn the last phase into a competition by counting the number of successful dive attempts.

MENTAL IMAGERY

In the sport of basketball, players routinely use mental imagery to enhance performance. A common example of this is when a player steps up to the free-throw line and, just before shooting, envisions the path of the ball as it approaches the basket and sinks over the front of the rim, swishing through the net. The sport of softball is quite different, but outfielders can use a similar imaging technique to make accurate throws to home plate, the bases, or other teammates. Although mental imagery can be used to enhance all outfield skills, drill 50: On the Money is specifically designed to improve throwing accuracy.

50 *On the Money*

Mental Skill   Mental imagery

Physical Skill   Outfield defense

Purpose   To help players develop accuracy when throwing from the outfield to infield targets

Implementation   Place a target at home plate. Players line up in left field. The coach hits from home plate, and the first player in line fields the ball and throws to the target at home plate. Before fielding, each player should create a mental image of herself throwing to the target (emphasizing the sound of the ball hitting the target). After one throw, the player goes to the back of the line. After each player has made 5 to 10 throws from left field, rotate to center field and then right field to repeat the drill. Upon returning to the back of the line, each player repeats her mental image in preparation for her next attempt.

Scoring   Each player counts the number of successful throws out of the total number of opportunities.

Variation   Players field the ball and throw to a target at home plate. If a player successfully hits the target, she rotates to another outfield position. One cycle is complete when a player rotates from left field to center to right to center and back to left field.

MENTAPHYSICAL WRAP-UP

The ability to stay in the present is one of the most important qualities an outfielder can possess. An increased distance from the action has the potential to decrease a player's ability to maintain focus for each play. There is a lot of time to think in the outfield, and players may become easily distracted by factors on and off the field. Therefore, outfielders should use a pre-performance routine to follow a sequence of thoughts and behaviors that will assure an optimal level of readiness for each play. This will help direct a player's attention to what she must do rather than what she did in the past, what a teammate did, or what the fans are doing. Drill 51: Head into the Play teaches outfielders the process of preparing for each pitch. Refer to figure 2.3 (page 37) for developing pre-performance routines.

51 *Head Into the Play*

Mental Skill   Energy regulation, concentration, confidence, mental imagery

Physical Skill   Outfield defense

Purpose   To help outfielders develop a pre-performance defensive routine to be used before the delivery of each pitch

Implementation   Conduct a controlled scrimmage, setting up various defensive situations. A pitcher simulates the pitching motion. The coach hits from home plate to the outfield. After each play is complete, all fielders rehearse a pre-performance routine. Elements of this routine may include the following:

- Relay the number of outs
- Scan the field in preparation for the next play
- Get into fielding position, directing focus to the infield
- Focus on the pitch

8

Pitching

Victory in the sport of softball requires winning each game within the game. For the team, softball is a game of runs. For the coach, softball is a game of strategy. For the defense, softball is a game of outs. For the offense, softball is a game of hits. For the pitcher, softball is a game of pitches. A pitcher throws each pitch in an attempt to dominate the batter—for every out, of every inning, of every game. Although strong hitting and a sound defense are very important for producing wins, ultimately, great teams rely on solid pitching to ensure performance excellence.

By virtue of her position, the pitcher assumes the role of field general. She is responsible for taking control, rallying her troops, and setting the tone of the game. In order to demonstrate effective leadership, a pitcher must sustain mental control over her emotions and physical control over her actions. How a pitcher conducts herself in the pitcher's circle strongly influences the thoughts and behaviors of her teammates and opponents. Exuding a confident demeanor has the potential to reinforce confidence in her teammates while simultaneously decreasing confidence in her opponents.

The position of pitcher is a unique one; she is the only true "offensive" player on both defensive and offensive sides of the game. The pitcher has the ability to control the tempo of the game by initiating the first movement of every play. If she does this effectively, the pitcher will create an advantage for herself and her teammates. For example, by maintaining a quick tempo, a pitcher may decrease a batter's chances of getting a hit by disrupting her batting routine. Minimizing the time taken in between pitches may force the batter to mentally and physically prepare at an uncomfortable pace. Conversely, throwing at a slower tempo may cause the defense to lose focus, which increases the chances for fielding errors. If defensive players are waiting for long periods, their muscles may become stiff. They may also lose concentration on the immediate situation and begin thinking about the past or future (this can induce distracting and negative thoughts).

Becoming a successful pitcher requires great accuracy, consistency, and discipline. Developing these qualities takes an immense amount of commitment; pitchers practice many more hours than their teammates, usually starting their practice long before the rest of the team arrives at the diamond. Because pitching is so demanding, a pitcher must have complete dedication to performance excellence.

While it is apparent that pitching involves a tremendous amount of mental and physical discipline, the pitcher's role involves more than just throwing the ball over the plate. To set a tone of domination and achieve greatness, a pitcher must learn how to strategize, make adjustments, concentrate, stay composed, be resilient, and dedicate herself to each and every pitch she delivers. How a pitcher thinks, acts, and manages herself in the pitcher's circle will determine whether she will maintain control of the game or be controlled by the game.

ENERGY REGULATION

Pitching requires a great amount of strength and endurance. Pitchers must learn how to work efficiently and effectively using the least possible amount of energy. Often, pitchers are expected to throw multiple innings or even several games in one day. This can be physically and mentally exhausting, and pitchers will sometimes run out of gas late in a game. As the saying goes, pitchers should "work smarter, not harder." Therefore, she must conserve her energy by directing and regulating her mental and physical energy.

Muscle Tension

A variety of factors influence the amount of tension a pitcher experiences during a game. In terms of speed and accuracy, a pitcher can expect the same results with varying amounts of muscle tension. Thus, to conserve energy, a pitcher should pitch in the most relaxed state that still allows for the best results. For example, muscling the ball over the plate will generate a great deal of speed, but if a pitcher relaxes and just uses her arm like a whip, she will conserve energy while achieving the same results. By remaining loose and allowing the body to move freely, pitching will require less effort, and the stamina needed for long bouts of pitching will be enhanced. Drill 52: Relax and Release is designed to help pitchers identify the minimal level of muscle tension necessary to achieve maximum speed and accuracy.

Managing Energy Level

When a pitcher is fatigued, she may experience difficulty throwing strikes or getting her pitches to work effectively. As previously mentioned, stamina and endurance are essential to dominating in the pitcher's circle. Therefore, a pitcher should engage in various types of endurance training. Although many coaches use distance running, rope jumping, cycling, and other activities to build players' endurance, the best way to train for a specific skill is by actually performing that skill. To become a better sprinter, one has to sprint. To become a better shooter, one has to shoot. To become a better pitcher, one has to pitch. While weightlifting and aerobic activities can be used to increase muscular strength and endurance, drill 53: Maxed Out is designed to help pitchers build strength and endurance specific to pitching. In addition, a pitcher's mental toughness will be challenged through the process of throwing for accuracy when fatigued.

52 *Relax and Release*

Mental Skill   Energy regulation

Physical Skill   Pitching

Purpose   To help pitchers develop kinesthetic awareness of muscle tension while performing proper pitching mechanics (this awareness will improve pitching speed and accuracy)

Implementation   Pitchers throw each type of pitch a total of 20 times in two sets of 10 each. Pitchers begin throwing pitches at a very high level of intensity by using all of their strength and effort to deliver the pitch. This will include an extensive amount of muscle tension in all major muscle groups, including the arms, legs, and torso. For the first set of 10 pitches, the pitchers should decrease the level of tension with each subsequent pitch. By the 10th pitch of the first set, the delivery should become almost effortless. The pitchers then perform the second set of 10 pitches at the lowest, most efficient, level of muscle tension (the level experienced on the 10th pitch of the first set).

Coaching Tips
- Remind the players that releasing muscle tension does not mean changing pitching mechanics.
- Ensure that players perform an adequate warm-up before initiating this drill.

53 *Maxed Out*

Mental Skill   Energy regulation

Physical Skill   Pitching

Purpose   To improve pitchers' accuracy when pitching under conditions in which stamina is being challenged

Implementation   Each pitcher works with a catcher. For 30 to 45 seconds, pitchers continuously deliver pitches without any breaks (speed drill). At the end of each session, catchers call a sequence of five specific pitches varied by type and location. Between the speed drill and sequence of five pitches, pitchers should take two shallow breaths followed by one deep breath, releasing tension in the shoulders during each exhalation. If pitchers accurately throw the sequence of five pitches to each designated location (judged by the catcher), they have successfully completed the drill. Pitchers who do not hit each specified location will repeat the speed drill and a new sequence of five different pitches until successful completion. Repeat until the pitcher hits each spot or has performed the speed drill a total of three to five times.

Scoring   Record the number of trials it takes to successfully complete the drill.

Coaching Tip   Adjust the number of pitches or cycles according to pitcher ability.

CONCENTRATION

Pitchers know that there is more to getting outs than simply throwing the ball across the plate. A pitcher must keep her opponents guessing and off balance by throwing a variety of pitches and pitch sequences. If a hitter knows what pitch is likely to be thrown, this will increase the probability that she will make solid contact with the ball. Eventually, hitters will become aware of the pitcher's tendencies. Thus, for the best results, the pitcher must be able to adjust the speed, movement, and sequence of pitches. Even the slightest pitching mistake can determine the outcome of a ball game. Therefore, it is absolutely essential that a pitcher maintain her focus before and during the delivery of each pitch. Drill 54: Centering the Signs is intended to challenge the pitcher to commit her attention to each pitch.

Attention Control

Before a pitch is thrown, most defensive players are prepared and in a ready position to field the ball. Pitchers, on the other hand, must wait until after the ball is pitched to shift into a fielding position. Not only does fielding the ball require a quick reaction, but a pitcher must also transition from an underhand to an overhand throwing motion in order to complete a play. The pitcher must perform three skills consecutively (pitching, fielding, throwing) in a very short period of time, often under three seconds. Sometimes this transition can be difficult, and pitchers will hesitate on the throw. Drill 55: Pitch, Field, Throw will allow pitchers to practice this sequence of actions.

54 *Centering the Signs*

Mental Skill Concentration

Physical Skill Pitching

Purpose To help pitchers improve their ability to focus attention on each pitch (and reduce the tendency to go through the motions without fully registering the catcher's signs)

Implementation Each pitcher throws two to three sequences of 10 pitches. During each sequence, the catcher signals the pitcher to throw varied pitches. The catcher should mix it up by changing pitches and pitch locations. The pitcher tries to completely register each sign by mentally talking herself through the process, answering two questions: What pitch am I throwing? and What location? From the time she receives the sign until the time the ball is released, the pitcher should be completely focused on the current pitch. For each sequence of 10 pitches, the pitcher should keep track of the number of times she successfully delivered the pitch without being distracted by other thoughts. If she recognizes that she has been distracted before the pitch is thrown, she should start over by requesting the catcher to repeat the signs.

Scoring At the end of each sequence, pitchers can record their scores to chart progress.

Coaching Tip To help pitchers avoid distracting thoughts, instruct them to mentally repeat the pitch to be thrown and the pitch location until the actual delivery of the pitch; for example, the pitcher may repeat in her mind, "Rise ball, high and inside."

Variation To increase the difficulty, the coach can provide distractions by making comments or having another player make comments throughout the pitching motion.

In eight seasons at the helm of University of Texas softball, head coach Connie Clark has lead the Longhorns to five NCAA Division I Tournament appearances, three Big 12 Conference Tournament titles, two Big 12 regular-season titles, and two Women's College World Series appearances. Coach Clark offers her favorite pitching drill, Stair Step Workout, which challenges pitchers to be able to hit intended locations with specific counts.

Connie Clark, head coach, University of Texas

Photo courtesy of UT Media Relations/New Media

Stair Step Workout

Mental Skill   Concentration

Physical Skill   Pitching

Purpose   To challenge pitchers to be able to hit the intended location with a specific count three times in a row

Implementation   Direct the pitcher to focus her attention on a designated pitch location. Then have pitchers throw three pitches per location for each pitch in their repertoire (for example, the first pitch they select will be thrown three times with a different count on each of the three pitches (fastball 0-0, fastball 1-2, fastball 0-2). The first pitch is thrown with an 0-0 count; the focus is on hitting a spot for a called strike. The second pitch is thrown with a 1-2 count; focus is on "missing" slightly. The third pitch is thrown with an 0-2 count; focus is to miss farther off the plate. The pitcher is successful if she is able to locate all three pitches to the proper location on the specific count.

Coaching Tips

- Use a hitter or tee to stand in the box to visually help the pitcher focus.
- If your goal is to keep track of pitch counts on a given day, this workout provides a minimum of three pitches per location or you can add pitches by adding "sets" (repeating drill several times) or requesting the pitcher hit the exact location before moving on.

55 *Pitch, Field, Throw*

Mental Skill Concentration

Physical Skill Pitching

Purpose To improve pitchers' ability to transition from pitching (using the underhand motion) to fielding and making a throw to a base (using the overhand motion)

Equipment Striped balls

Implementation Position an infielder at each base. The coach is positioned in the batter's box with a bucket of striped softballs. Pitchers take turns throwing one pitch to a catcher. After the pitch crosses the plate, the coach hits a ground ball to the pitcher. The pitcher must recognize the number of stripes on the ball and respond by throwing to the appropriate base (one stripe = first base, two stripes = second base, three stripes = third base). While fielding the ball, pitchers should say a cue or trigger word related to the number of stripes (such as "one" for a throw to first base). Rotate pitchers after each play. Repeat 10 to 15 times for each pitcher.

Scoring Record the number of successful throws to bases.

Coaching Tip Encourage pitchers to play aggressively when fielding the ball; the more game-like the better.

COACH'S FAVORITE DRILL

Photo courtesy of Michigan State University Athletics

Coach Jacquie Joseph has led the Michigan State University Spartans softball team for 10 years, taking her team to three NCAA regional tournaments. Coach Joseph has published several books and videotapes, including her own drill book, *Defensive Softball Drills* (for more information, contact her on the Web at www.jacquiejoseph.com). STRIKE Her Out is Coach Joseph's favorite competitive drill for pitchers.

Jacquie Joseph, head coach, Michigan State University

STRIKE Her Out

Mental Skill   Concentration

Physical Skill   Pitching

Purpose   To increase pitchers' ability to regulate attention style in the face of competition

Implementation   Two pitchers throw side by side with two catchers. The first pitcher starts by calling the location of the pitch she would like to throw. For example, "high inside" or numbers can be used to identify zone locations. Then she throws that pitch. If she hits her spot, judged by the catcher, the second pitcher attempts to throw that same pitch. Instruct the challenger to focus her attention by going from broad external (thinking about the called pitch and how she will make her delivery) to narrow external (thinking only about the actual delivery). The goal is to eliminate the distraction of competition by focusing solely on that particular pitch. If the second pitcher hits the spot, the first pitcher goes again; if the second pitcher misses, she gets the letter *S*. If the first pitcher does not hit the correct spot, then the second pitcher gets to take a turn and call a pitch. The pitcher who spells *STRIKE* first loses the competition.

Variations

- Increase the difficulty by requiring that the pitch be within a one-half-ball margin from the spot.
- Decrease the difficulty by allowing the pitch to have a two-ball-width margin for hitting the spot.

CONFIDENCE

Composure is probably the most pivotal psychological skill for a pitcher to develop because it will help her maintain mental and physical control of a game. To put it simply, composure refers to the ability to be confident, resilient, and controlled while performing. Staying composed in the face of competitive pressure means dealing with adversity. For instance, pitchers are often frustrated by decisions made by home plate umpires. When a pitcher allows the umpire and others to know she is frustrated, this can hinder her performance. Responding in this manner will elicit negative thoughts that have a direct impact on subsequent performance and behavior.

Maintaining composure is more important for a pitcher than for any other defensive position. All pitchers experience a wide array of emotional responses during the course of a game, from frustration, to disappointment, to satisfaction, to triumph. How a pitcher interprets and reacts to these emotions, as shown through her mannerisms, will have an impact on her execution, and subsequently, on the performance of others. For example, if the opposing team is consistently making solid contact with the ball, a pitcher may become frustrated. If she shows this frustration through nonverbal behaviors (e.g., anguished facial expressions) and body language (e.g., poor posture), the opposing team will read this message and become more confident. In addition, her own teammates may lose faith in her ability and may focus on her poor attitude, distracting them from their own mission and responsibilities. Regardless of frustration, intimidation, or elation, a pitcher should keep her feelings guarded. Sport scientists have documented that elite athletes possess a tremendous ability to maintain control over their emotions. Therefore, a pitcher must be able to mask her feelings and sustain her game face, her game presence, and her game composure. Drill 56: Cool Pose challenges a pitcher's ability to do that.

56 *Cool Pose*

Mental Skill   Confidence

Physical Skill   Pitching

Purpose   To help pitchers develop the three Cs (confidence, composure, competitiveness) by modeling confident behavior during pitching practice

Implementation   Conduct regular pitching drills. Instruct the pitchers to exude confidence through body language and by modeling the three Cs during the drills. Presence in the pitcher's circle should include a competitive, serious, and confident demeanor. This might include good posture, shoulders back, head high, and eyes focused on the catcher. Don't allow players to drag their feet or hang their head. Players should use affirmations to reinforce the physical elements of body language throughout each drill. Positive affirmations for pitchers may include "This is a strike," "I've got your number," or "I'm in control."

Coaching Tips   Encourage players to use affirmations and positive, confident body language to develop a "love to pitch, ready to field, going to throw a strike" attitude.

MENTAL IMAGERY

Similar to serving a volleyball, pitching a softball represents a "closed" skill. It is the only skill in softball where the performer is not reacting to a play but is instead initiating an action. Therefore, imagery can be a very effective tool for enhancing pitching performance. The best way for players to learn basic imagery is by seeing themselves perform. A quick source for doing this is a mirror. When a pitcher performs in front of a mirror, this provides her with an image that she can then use to visualize her motion. The pictures created in her mind enable her to practice the perfect execution of various pitching techniques on and off the field. Drill 57: See a Strike is a basic external imagery drill for pitchers.

It is not uncommon for a pitcher to experience difficulty with a specific aspect of her pitching. For example, her rise ball may be flat or her curveball may lack movement. When a minor adjustment is necessary, the solution to the problem may not be obvious. Astute coaches will instruct pitchers on how to make corrections, but sometimes pitchers will find it difficult to adjust. When performing a skill, it is sometimes challenging to pinpoint the exact source of the problem. Drill 58: Process Versus Product teaches pitchers how to improve technique by recognizing specified movements kinesthetically.

See the pitch *before* you throw it by visualizing the motions.

Once a pitcher has a basic sense of how mental imagery can be used and has developed a kinesthetic awareness of her pitching movements, she will be ready to use a more advanced form of imagery. Drill 59: Positive Pitching for Perfection is designed to help pitchers develop pitch control. The goal of this drill is to be able to deliver a series of specified pitches integrating mental imagery between each delivery.

57 See a Strike

Mental Skill   Mental imagery

Physical Skill   Pitching

Purpose   To help pitchers learn how to use imagery to perfect pitching mechanics

Implementation   The pitcher performs her pitching motion in front of a mirror. After completing each pitch, the pitcher closes her eyes and imagines herself performing the pitch as if she is watching herself on video. Repeat 20 to 30 times.

Coaching Tips   Ensure that pitchers use varied pitches and that they watch the differences in delivery for each type.

58 Process Versus Product

Mental Skill   Mental imagery

Physical Skill   Pitching

Purpose   To help pitchers improve pitching mechanics and establish body awareness by paying attention to specified body segments throughout the throwing motion

Implementation   The pitcher stands 10 to 15 feet in front of a fence or a screen with a bucket of approximately 20 balls. She selects two specific fundamentals to practice throughout the drill, such as wrist snap and foot placement. The pitcher will throw a total of three buckets of balls, directing her attention to one particular fundamental (body part) at a time. While throwing the balls from the first bucket, the pitcher devotes her attention to the first fundamental (e.g., wrist snap); during the second bucket of balls, she directs her attention to the second fundamental (e.g., foot placement). To help develop an awareness of each particular body part, the pitcher alternates throwing pitches with her eyes open and closed. For the final bucket of balls, the pitcher alternates her focus back and forth between the two body parts. Success is determined by proper execution of the isolated portion of the skill, not the outcome of the pitch.

59 *Positive Pitching for Perfection*

Mental Skill Mental imagery

Physical Skill Pitching

Purpose To help pitchers develop pitching accuracy and control using mental imagery

Implementation Near the end of pitching practice, the coach selects a sequence of three pitches, such as the following:

- Rise ball, high and inside
- Change-up, low and outside
- Curveball or screwball, low and inside

Each pitcher must accurately perform the sequence of pitches three times in a row (total of nine pitches). Before the delivery of each pitch, the pitcher should visualize the particular pitch to the desired location and repeat a positive self-statement (such as the following examples).

- I will hit my spot.
- This is my best pitch.
- I'm in control.
- Attack the zone.

If the pitcher misses the intended target, she must repeat the drill beginning with the first pitch in the sequence. The catcher judges the accuracy of each pitch.

Scoring Each pitcher keeps track of the number of times she had to repeat the drill sequence.

Coaching Tips When pitches are not working, this drill can become grueling. Continue to emphasize the use of positive self-talk and the concept of mental toughness.

MENTAPHYSICAL WRAP-UP

The position of pitcher in the game of softball has a unique status. The pitcher is the leader of the defense. She is involved with every batter and participates in every play. The physical and mental skills necessary to perform well cannot be overemphasized. A pitcher may throw a great game one day and have a poor outing the next. The ability to be consistent, physically and mentally, should be a high priority. By using the various psychological skills presented in this chapter, a pitcher should be able to develop into a more consistent player, and consequently, a more successful player. Drill 60: The Great ESCAPE is designed to teach pitchers how to integrate many of the necessary skills into a pre-performance routine. This routine should be used before the delivery of each pitch in practice and competition. See figure 2.3 (page 37) to help pitchers develop their own pre-performance routine.

60 The Great ESCAPE

Mental Skill Energy regulation, concentration, confidence, imagery

Physical Skill Pitching

Purpose To practice using a pre-performance routine that will mentally and physically prepare the pitcher to be more consistent and successful

Implementation Set up a scrimmage by dividing the team in half. Throughout the scrimmage, the pitchers should perform a pre-performance routine before each pitch. The sample routine denoted by the acronym *ESCAPE* includes the following elements:

- Evaluate—evaluate the situation (outs, runners, batter tendencies)
- Signs—read the signs from the catcher
- Cue—direct attention to a specific cue (the pitch to be thrown)
- Assess—assess your energy level
- Pitch—throw the pitch
- Evaluate—evaluate the effectiveness of the previous pitch and repeat the initial evaluation procedure

Coaching Tips Pitchers can create their own acronyms to help remind them of the sequence of behaviors they will perform before each pitch.

9

Catching

Catching is one of the most important defensive positions. While the pitcher's field presence is obvious by virtue of her central field position, the catcher's field presence is less noticeable, but just as important. Although she is not the initiator of action, the catcher is directly and indirectly involved in every play. Other defenders are responsible for taking action after the ball is contacted, but the catcher takes an active role both before and after the delivery of each pitch.

The catcher is a quiet accomplice to the pitcher, actively participating in the negotiation and decision making process before each pitch. After the ball is contacted, the catcher shifts to a more vocal role. In a bunt, passed ball, or pop-up situation, where she is directly involved in the play, her vocal presence is evident as she orchestrates the play by calling for the ball, communicating with teammates, and completing the play. In situations where she is not directly involved, such as a grounder on the infield or a fly ball to the outfield, the catcher remains active in the play by verbally directing her teammates. The catcher has a unique vantage point because she is the only defensive player who faces all of her teammates and sees the entire playing field, much like a quarterback in football. In order to direct her teammates, the catcher must know every detail of the immediate situation; after the ball is contacted, she must scan the field, anticipate the outcome, and make a quick decision to help guide her teammates toward the correct response.

To perform this commanding role effectively, a catcher must demonstrate exceptional mental and physical toughness. She must be a rock for her team because she bears the weight of numerous responsibilities. Most great catchers have a sturdy physique with tremendous upper and lower body strength. Although catching the ball is her first priority, she must also become proficient at framing and blocking pitches. Furthermore, to make strong and accurate throws, the catcher must coordinate complex movements, quickly transferring the ball from the glove to her throwing hand while getting out of the squatting position. Her responsibilities are even more challenging because she must maneuver herself (while weighted down by bulky protective gear) to avoid interference with the batter or umpire.

On defense, a catcher is continuously thinking and strategizing. She must maintain complete focus throughout the entire course of an inning. While most defensive players have opportunities to take brief mental breaks between pitches, the catcher does not. She is constantly processing information, making decisions, and preparing for the next play. Aside from the pitcher, the catcher is the only player who must refocus her thoughts before and after every pitch. This refocusing requires that the catcher process all relevant information to decide which pitch should be thrown, including information about the hitter, the pitcher, the inning, the score, the number of outs, the count, and the base runners. The catcher's goal is to put her team in the best position to get an out or somehow create an advantage over the opponent. For example, with a runner on third base and less than two outs, it is important to keep the ball on the infield to prevent the run from scoring. Therefore, knowing that a high pitch will give the hitter a better opportunity to hit the ball out of the infield, a catcher is not likely to call for a rise ball. In contrast, a different defensive player in this same situation, such as the shortstop, does not necessarily have to think about the details associated with each pitch. For the entire at-bat, the shortstop can focus solely on fielding the ball, holding the runner at third, and throwing to first base.

All great catchers have the ability to communicate effectively. The catcher is in charge of delivering and relaying messages between teammates, coaches, and game officials. The most important line of communication is between the pitcher and catcher because they are the only two players who are mentally and physically involved in every play. Trust, respect, and confidence are at the core of this relationship. While the pitcher works at her own pace, setting the game tempo, her actions are dependent upon the catcher. The catcher must pay attention to various factors to help the pitcher maintain a comfortable rhythm and maximize performance. A catcher must be in tune with how the pitcher thinks, what pitches she likes to throw, the sequence she likes to throw them in, and what pitches are working on that particular day. In addition, the catcher is expected to pay attention to how the pitcher is feeling. An occasional trip to the pitcher's circle is necessary to provide the pitcher with support, calm her down, or pick her up when things aren't going well. If the pitcher is having a horrible day, the catcher can reinforce the pitcher's confidence by keeping her focused on what she is doing well and on what she can adjust to perform better. A catcher serves as an on-field support system for the pitcher, assisting with and reinforcing her game management.

Good communication is extremely important for the catcher, whether you're talking to the pitcher or directing fielders.

Along with developing a good working relationship with the pitcher, a catcher must build a strong rapport with coaches, teammates, and umpires. She may work with the coach to call pitches or to relay information about defensive positioning. As the director of plays, she must also earn the trust of her teammates so they have confidence in her ability to make decisions and lead the team. In addition, a catcher has a unique relationship with the home plate umpire. The catcher is the person who shields the umpire from being hit by a pitched ball. She must acquire the respect of umpires in case she wants to negotiate a call or inquire about the strike zone. She has to get a read on the umpire because some umpires are offended easily and do not like it when players ask questions. Developing a good rapport with the home plate umpire could influence calls in her team's favor.

Ultimately, the role of the catcher is the most complex. She is involved in every play; she calls the pitches, directs the infield, and takes cues from the coaching staff. Thus, learning to integrate relevant mental skills will benefit the person who is responsible for this important assignment.

ENERGY REGULATION

As noted, catching is a very physically demanding position. Imagine how your legs would feel after doing 15 minutes of squats, let alone 2 to 3 hours of squats. If the body is not trained for this type of activity, muscle soreness and fatigue are inevitable. In addition, catching involves a unique strength that is not only physical, but also mental. A catcher must sacrifice her body to defend the plate. This requires a mind-set in which the catcher feels impenetrable, likening herself to a brick or steel wall. She wears protective gear for a reason; pitches are thrown at average speeds of 60 miles per hour, batters swing at pitches with all of their might, and runners who attempt to score may collide with the catcher as she protects the plate. The mental and physical demands of this position elicit changes in the amount of energy used in various game situations.

Managing Energy Level

When a game is on the line and one or more runners are in scoring position, a catcher may experience emotional changes that cause fluctuations in energy. If the catcher becomes overexcited or worried, she may lose her competitive focus or experience a moment of doubt. Her muscles may tighten, causing jerky and uncoordinated movements or delayed reactions. Drill 61: Knock It Down is designed to help a catcher learn to channel this energy and to help her feel comfortable calling the best pitch (even a pitch that is difficult to handle) when runners are in scoring position.

61 Knock It Down

Mental Skill   Energy regulation

Physical Skill   Catching

Purpose   To increase a catcher's ability to regulate arousal levels when runners are in scoring position

Implementation   Players line up at third base to take turns as the base runner. Instruct catchers to call pitches that are risky (more difficult to handle) with runners in scoring position (e.g., change-ups, drop balls, and so forth). Catchers take turns blocking pitches, rotating after every 5 pitches. Between each pitch, the catcher should take a short, but slow breath. Each catcher will block a total of 40 to 50 pitches. The object is to block the ball in order to keep the runner at third base from scoring. The runner takes a lead, and if the ball gets by the catcher, the runner decides whether or not to run to home plate. On a passed ball, the pitcher should cover home plate, and the catcher should complete the play by trying to throw the runner out at home.

COACH'S FAVORITE DRILL

Coach John Reeves is the first assistant on the UC Berkeley Bears softball squad and has been with the program for 12 years (winning the NCAA Division I national championship in 2002 and competing again for the title in 2003). Coach Reeves works with pitchers and catchers. He created the Conditioning for Passed Balls drill for players to work on conditioning and on developing the skills needed to recover from a catching error.

Photo courtesy of UC Berkeley Media Relations

John Reeves, first assistant, University of California at Berkeley

Conditioning for Passed Balls

Mental Skill   Energy regulation

Physical Skill   Catching

Purpose   To increase stamina and help catchers learn to regulate energy when retrieving passed balls

Implementation   Several balls are placed near the backstop behind the catcher. The catcher assumes her normal receiving position. The pitcher simulates a pitch (without a ball). The catcher sprints and slides to one of the balls placed at the backstop. She must then make an accurate throw to the pitcher covering home plate. The catcher takes two deep, controlled breaths while getting back to her position. Repeat until all balls are fielded. If the catcher makes a bad throw, or the pitcher is late covering home plate or misses a throw from the catcher, a ball may be added to the backstop.

CONCENTRATION

When a runner is in scoring position, a good catcher will do anything in her power to stop the runner from crossing home plate. If a pitch is thrown wildly, she will use her body like a wall to keep the ball in front of her. When a runner is approaching home and a throw is coming in from the outfield, a catcher must protect the plate as if it were her fortress. She must stand her ground knowing that a collision is probable. Regardless of the situation, great catching requires an attitude in which the catcher is willing to sacrifice her body for the sake of the team. In order to protect the plate, a catcher must exhibit a wealth of confidence. Although her primary focus must always be on the ball (narrow external), she must maintain an awareness of the approaching runner. If she is distracted by the runner before cleanly fielding the ball, successful completion of the play is compromised and a run is likely to score. Drill 62: Stop the Score teaches a catcher how to concentrate effectively while covering home plate.

Catching for long periods of time can become monotonous and tiring. It is not uncommon for a catcher to begin calling the same pattern of pitches. Although the situation changes for each pitch, catchers sometimes fall into routines. This is rarely helpful in competitive situations. If a catcher allows herself to lose focus with a runner on base, she might be caught on her heels if the base runner steals. Coaches will typically respond to this behavior by making a comment such as "Wake up" or "Don't get caught on your heels." When the bases are occupied, a catcher must use a narrow external attention style to catch the ball, while still using her peripheral vision to sustain field awareness. Though good communication among players is pivotal, a catcher should not rely solely on her teammates to read a situation such as a runner stealing a base. Drill 63: Catch the Steal will help catchers learn to anticipate the steal by working on catching the pitch, scanning the field, and making a throw.

62 *Stop the Score*

Mental Skill Concentration

Physical Skill Catching

Purpose To develop catchers' ability to concentrate effectively while receiving a throw from the outfield with a runner approaching home plate

Implementation The catcher is in position behind the plate. Players line up at second base to take turns as the base runner. Outfielders assume their primary positions. The pitcher simulates a pitch from the pitcher's circle. Upon the simulated delivery, the runner takes her lead from second base. The coach then hits to the outfield from home plate. The base runner responds to the outfield hit by advancing toward home and forcing a throw to the plate. Knowing that the runner is coming home, the catcher can plan ahead for the play at home. This limits the number of decisions she must make, thus decreasing the complexity and allowing her to focus on making the catch at home. While the ball and the runner are both coming toward home plate, the catcher should repeat a phrase to herself in order to direct her attention toward successful completion of the play (for example, "Knock it down," "Come at me," or "Bring it home").

63 Catch the Steal

Mental Skill Concentration

Physical Skill Catching

Purpose To improve catchers' ability to quickly shift attention during the pitching-catching sequence when runners are on the bases

Implementation The catcher is in position behind the plate. Base runners occupy first and second base. Infielders play their respective positions. The pitcher will deliver a pitch. Before the pitch, the coach holds up a number of fingers (one, two, or fist):

- One: runner on first steals second
- Two: runner on second steals third
- Fist: both runners steal

The runner who is not assigned to steal should practice taking an aggressive lead. The catcher must catch the pitch (narrow external attention), scan the bases (broad external attention), recognize which runner is stealing, and throw the ball to the correct base (narrow external attention).

Scoring Record the number of times the catcher throws out a base runner.

CONFIDENCE

The role of the catcher is quite diverse. She is responsible for many facets of the game. This requires the catcher not only to be able to focus her attention effectively, but also to trust in her ability to successfully perform her role. During tough situations that occur throughout a game, such as having runners in scoring position or getting behind in the count, a catcher may play timidly. A catcher who is fearful will call pitches that are easy to block rather than choosing the most appropriate pitch to dominate the hitter at that moment. For example, with a runner on third base, a catcher may avoid calling a drop ball or a change-up because she is afraid of a passed ball (which could result in a run for the opponent). This fear can be addressed directly by using drill 64: Steel Wall.

Sometimes catchers will lose their confidence and hesitate when making quick and critical decisions. An example of this is when the catcher is responsible for fielding a bunt with runners on base. Coaches often harp on players for not fielding the bunt quickly enough to get the lead runner. Drill 65: See the Stripes will allow catchers to practice fielding the bunt, making a quick decision, and responding to the play.

64 Steel Wall

Mental Skill Confidence

Physical Skill Catching

Purpose To develop a catcher's confidence in her ability to block bad pitches

Implementation A pitcher (any player can perform this role) throws bad pitches. Catchers take turns blocking five pitches. Each catcher should repeat a self-talk statement that helps her create a mental picture of something that cannot be penetrated (for example, "steel wall"). After five pitches, rotate to the next catcher.

Scoring The first catcher to successfully block 30 balls by keeping the ball in front of her wins the drill.

65 See the Stripes

Mental Skill Confidence

Physical Skill Catching

Purpose To improve a catcher's ability to quickly field a bunt and throw to the appropriate base

Equipment Striped softballs

Implementation Position an infielder at each base. The pitcher will throw a pitch from the pitcher's circle to the catcher. The coach stands in the batter's box with a bucket of striped softballs. After the pitch crosses the plate, the coach lays down a bunt (randomly selecting one of the striped balls). The catcher must quickly field the bunt, determine the number of stripes on the ball, and make a throw to the corresponding base (one stripe = first base, two stripes = second base, three stripes = third base). Instruct the catcher to identify the number of stripes as soon as possible and call out the number of the base where the ball will be thrown. This will work as a concentration trigger word and also communicate to the infielder that the ball is coming.

Scoring Record the number of correct and accurate throws.

MENTAL IMAGERY

Learning and performing complex sport skills is a continuous challenge for athletes. Great coaches spend the majority of their time teaching and refining mechanics and fundamentals. Because the catching position involves dynamic and changing tasks, it is difficult to use mental imagery to account for every situation. Nonetheless, mental imagery can be used if the catcher is having trouble in a certain situation. For example, she can imagine herself as a steel wall to help her block balls at the plate; she can imagine herself making a throw on a runner who is stealing a base; or she can imagine herself guarding home plate as the ball and a runner are approaching simultaneously. The best use of imagery for a catcher is to improve technique. For drill 66: Perfect Reflection, the catcher is simply seeing herself perform her role correctly and then re-creating that image in her mind.

This drill can be specifically adapted to help catchers with technique when responding to various situations.

66 *Perfect Reflection*

Mental Skill Mental imagery

Physical Skill Catching

Purpose   To improve catching technique through immediate feedback and mental imagery

Equipment   Full-length mirror

Implementation   The catcher works on proper catching and throwing techniques in front of a mirror (calling signs, receiving the pitch, throwing out the runner, blocking the plate). After completing each play, the catcher closes her eyes and imagines herself performing the skills as if she is watching herself on video. Repeat 20 to 30 times.

MENTAPHYSICAL WRAP-UP

Every defensive position requires specialized training, but the role of catcher has more demands than any other position. Therefore, the use of specific mental training strategies can only serve to help a catcher meet the requirements necessary for performance excellence. Sport psychologists have discovered that pre-performance routines provide a great source of structure for behavior and are effective for developing consistency in mental discipline, decision making, and physical performance. Catchers can create a pre-performance routine to avoid feeling overwhelmed by their numerous responsibilities. This will allow them to develop a sequence of behaviors that, with practice, will become automated and reduce the complexity of this demanding position. Drill 67: SORT It Out provides the catcher with a sample pre-performance routine for her demanding role. See figure 2.3 (page 37) to help catchers create their own pre-performance routines.

67   *SORT It Out*

Mental Skill   Energy regulation, concentration, confidence, mental imagery

Physical Skill   Catching

Purpose   To practice using a pre-performance routine that will mentally and physically prepare the catcher to be more consistent and successful

Implementation   Set up a scrimmage by dividing the team in half. Throughout the scrimmage, the catcher should perform a pre-performance routine before each pitch. The sample routine denoted by the acronym *SORT* includes the following elements:

- Scan—scan the field and evaluate the situation (outs, runners, batter tendencies)
- Organize—based on the evaluation, organize your thoughts
- Review—affirm and make the pitch selection based on the evaluation
- Target—give the signal and set up the target

10

Team Building

Playing competitive softball is a worthwhile experience for young women. There are unique challenges such as daily practices, time spent traveling, difficult weather conditions, and physical conditioning sessions. On the other hand, there are great opportunities that come with such challenges, including getting to know teammates and coaches, learning leadership skills, and sharing experiences with others who have similar goals.

To overcome the lows, relish the highs, and truly achieve greatness, coaches and players must come together and form a unit. The epitome of team cohesion is when a common goal is finally achieved and each team member experiences the same thoughts, feelings, and emotions. This is the moment of glory that comes after an intense victory, a great play, or a game-winning hit. It cannot be reproduced and it quickly fades away, but the memory and the feelings that accompany those moments last forever in the minds and hearts of those who share in the experience.

Sports can be divided into three categories: coactive, interactive, and coactive-interactive. Coactive sports, typically described as *individual sports*, require no interdependence among players. These sports include bowling, golf, and tennis. Interactive sports, on the other hand, involve a significant amount of interdependence among the players. The actions of one player depend on the actions of her teammates in order to be successful. Examples of interactive sports include basketball, hockey, and soccer. Softball falls into the category of coactive-interactive sports because it involves both types of activities—individual activities and activities that require interaction among team members. Although softball players clearly need to possess skills that are not dependent on their teammates (e.g., batting ability), they must also be able to perform skills that require team interaction (e.g., turning a double play). Because softball does require team members to rely on one another for precise execution, team building is a central theme among coaches. The importance of team building cannot be overstated. The fundamental goal is to increase team cohesion so that players and coaches can communicate effectively and work together to achieve a common goal.

COMMUNICATION

Effective communication is one of the most important components of overall team cohesion and success. Most players will agree that the best coaches are the ones who have the ability to communicate well with the players. This includes providing instruction and praise, having a sense of humor, and being consistent. Communication gives the coach a window into the players' needs. This section provides coaches with some guidelines for effective communication and strategies for improving team communication.

For communication to be effective, the messages being sent must be clear and direct. It is a terrible feeling to be misunderstood. In pressure situations, coaches are often as intense as the players (if not more intense). Many coaches have a tendency to raise their voice and use exaggerated mannerisms in these situations. Players who are sensitive to these changes in coach behavior may direct more attention to *how* their coach is delivering the message than to *what* their coach is actually trying to convey. Some players may even interpret their coach's behavior as threatening and may lose their focus and confidence. Therefore, coaches must be aware of how their words and actions affect players; they must be sure that players do not take the messages personally and that players understand the meaning in every message. Coaches and players need to completely understand each other's methods of communication in order to ensure a productive working environment.

A hallmark of good instruction is constructive criticism. This is when a coach provides constructive information that teaches players what to correct and how to correct it. In addition to explaining how to make a correction, coaches should also offer players a reason for why the correction is necessary. Not only will this help persuade players to make an adjustment, but it will also provide them with a deeper understanding of various game strategies. When critiquing a player's behavior, it is imperative that the coach critiques the action and not the person. A player cannot change who she is, but she does have the ability to change her behaviors. Criticism aimed at a personal level will undermine the player's confidence. For example, if a coach responds to a fielding error by asking the player, "What were you thinking?" or by saying, "That was a stupid mistake," the player may begin to question her overall ability. Instead, a coach should respond with constructive comments such as, "Next time, watch the ball all the way into the glove" or "Charge the ball to take away the bad hop." This will communicate what needs to be corrected without jeopardizing the player's self-esteem. Most players will already recognize their own mistakes, they need to be acknowledged but not negatively reinforced by the coaching staff.

Several simple strategies can be used to improve team communication. One-on-one communication has been shown to be much more effective than group instruction. Research has shown that players who receive more individual feedback from their coaches improve more, perform better, and rate their coaches as more effective. Once players learn the general techniques for skills such as hitting and fielding, they will greatly benefit from one-on-one instruction. This type of instruction allows the coach to individualize feedback to accommodate a player's style of play (taking into account relevant factors such as body type and current level of ability).

Open Door Policy

Many coaches believe in having an open-door policy. However, coaches often have different ideas of what this policy entails. In addition, just because coaches believe they have an open-door policy, this doesn't necessarily mean that their players perceive it the same way. An open-door policy should be just that—the coach's door is open when players feel a need to talk. Although it would be nice if coaches could drop everything each time a player walked through the office door, this is not realistic. Sometimes coaches are bogged down with paperwork and other off-the-field duties. In any case, the coach should always acknowledge the player, tell her whether or not it is a good time to talk, and if it is not, give her another time that she can come back. If she does not come back to the office, the coach should follow up on her status and find out if she still needs advice. This demonstrates that the coach cares about the player, is interested in her, and believes that her concerns are worth the coach's time.

Evaluating the Coach

Although players are rarely given the opportunity to evaluate their coach's performance, this is an effective way to encourage two-way communication. When given the opportunity, players can provide valuable information. Evidence suggests that coaches are often inaccurate in their perceptions of how much and what types of feedback they are providing to players. Coaches tend to be overly optimistic; in other words, they assess themselves as giving more feedback than is actually given. They also perceive this feedback as being more positive than it actually is. When working with 15 or more players, it can be difficult for coaches to remember the amount and type of feedback provided to each player. Therefore, coaches must pay attention to the way they provide feedback to make sure they are accommodating the needs of all players.

Active Listening

Finally, because communication is a two-way process, coaches should examine their listening skills. Active listening can be a helpful strategy to improve communication. This method encourages the listener to paraphrase the meaning of the message. For example, when a player voices a concern, the coach should listen and then reiterate the message to ensure that the intent was fully understood. Coaches must also allow players to voice how they feel without becoming defensive. Some players may say things that are difficult to hear, but if they are taking the risk to tell their coach what they are thinking or how they are feeling, then the coach should be willing to hear them out. If a coach turns a player away or does not make an effort to truly listen, this will decrease the player's respect for the coach and may decrease her willingness to share with the coach in the future. The players are the ones who get out there and perform. So if a coach wants players to perform their best, then she must work hard to meet their needs and keep them satisfied. To have a true open-door policy, not only must a coach be available when needed, but the coach must also be able to listen despite what a player might share. Coaches must also remember that effective communication requires that they behave in a consistent manner both on and off the field. This consistency will bolster team cohesion. Figure 10.1 offers some basic elements of effective and ineffective communication.

Figure 10.1   Effective and Ineffective Communication

Effective	Ineffective
Active listener	Poor listening skills
Open-door policy	Unavailable to players
Constructive feedback	Punitive feedback
Consistent verbal and nonverbal cues	Contradictory verbal and nonverbal cues
Direct eye contact	Avoidant eye contact

PLAYING AS A TEAM

Coaches use the terms *team cohesion, team chemistry*, and *team harmony* to express the same sentiment—they want their players to interact as a collective unit. This usually involves two things. First and foremost, coaches want their players to play well together and demonstrate effective teamwork. Second, coaches hope that their players enjoy each other's company. Although it is not absolutely necessary for teammates to be friends in order to perform well, communication is enhanced when team members get along with each other. This is obvious in practice when the players partner up for drills. They tend to work with the teammates who are their friends because they are more comfortable with each other (and because it is simply more fun). If the members of a team like each other, and like to be with each other, the team is more likely to communicate effectively on the field and enjoy practice time. This will lead to a more productive environment.

One of the most difficult tasks college coaches face is creating a cohesive team environment. Often, one player can mean the difference between having a cohesive unit or a team divided. Teresa Wilson, head coach of the University of Washington Huskies, described the importance of team cohesion: ". . . cohesion enables them [the team] to function with complete chemistry as one." That is the ultimate goal when coaching players in a team sport—getting them to work together so well that they operate as a unit rather than a group of individuals. Whichever term is used, the meaning is clear: team cohesion, primarily in the form of teamwork, is an important ingredient to reaching performance excellence in the sport of softball.

According to Jeff Janssen, a sport psychology practitioner who works with collegiate softball teams, effective teamwork leads to success, and subsequently, satisfaction. When a team can come together as one, playing the game becomes easy. This is evident on the field when all players are communicating with one another. When this occurs, relaying messages does not take as much effort. If every player is doing her part, then one player does not have to pick up the slack for her teammates. When only two or three players are communicating on the field, these players will be expending extra energy for those who are not doing their part. Unfortunately, having to expend extra energy on these responsibilities will decrease the amount of effort these players can direct toward completing the physical and mental tasks related to the game. They may even become overly concerned, or even distracted, by what their teammates are *not* doing, which also has the potential to take away from their game focus. Over the course of the game, these players will become fatigued and even frustrated with carrying the weight of their teammates. When they become completely drained and cannot continue to give, all forms of communication will suffer, and team performance will decrease. In contrast, if every player contributes by doing her part, communicating will seem easy. The team will then function as a unit, and each player will be able to apply her energy and completely focus her efforts toward achieving a common team goal. Margo Jonker, head coach at Central Michigan University, describes how to achieve team success: "When each student-athlete reaches her potential, when the team is always put first, and when each player knows and accepts her role on the team, the team will reach its potential."

Team cohesion makes softball more enjoyable and sets the stage for the team to experience success. Success leads to winning, and winning is a very satisfying feeling. That is one reason why players choose to compete—winning feels good. Furthermore, players enjoy developing close relationships with teammates and coaches. The bonds that players develop when participating on teams are unique and can last long after a season or playing career is over. It is rare to have a situation in which a group of people share so much time, expend so much energy, and sacrifice so many of their personal desires to contribute to a common goal. For the sport of softball, it is fair to say that team cohesion is the foundation of performance excellence. So if cohesion is the foundation, what is the framework for a cohesive team?

GUIDELINES FOR COHESION

Although it would be easy to compose an extended list of factors that positively influence team cohesion, there are a few major guidelines. The following sections describe ways that coaches can build and maintain team cohesion.

Promote a Dream Goal or Mission

Coaches must be able to sell a dream goal or mission. They must generate enthusiasm and conviction among team members that this goal is worthy of achievement. Players need to know that in order to reach the goal, everyone must make an investment. A coach can keep the goal in the forefront of the players' minds by continually reminding them of what they can achieve and what it will feel like when they finally achieve it. Winning can be used as an example—the coach should ask the players to recall what it felt like when they won a really close or meaningful game. Ask them to think about how they want to feel after they play. Ask them what they are willing to do in order to make this feeling a reality. In addition, coaches must convey that they are willing to do anything on their part to achieve this goal. If the coach demonstrates a true willingness to sacrifice, the players are more likely to follow suit. Thus, it truly becomes a team goal. See figure 10.2 for ways to create a team mission.

Team cohesion soars when the mission, or dream goal, of the team is given priority over any conflict that emerges. One way to quickly destroy team chemistry is to emphasize the problems and minimize the mission. Instead, coaches should keep the players focused on their commitment to the goal. Teams come together when goals are met. Reminding players of the feeling associated with goal accomplishment will promote the sense of togetherness that occurs when a goal is actually reached. When adversity does

Figure 10.2 Creating a Team Mission

Creating a common mission gives your team something to focus on throughout the season. It provides a sense of purpose, which can be continually reinforced all season long. This is also a great activity for refining team goals for the season.

If you are concerned about some athletes not contributing, pose these questions and have them write their responses individually before generating the discussion. This guarantees that everyone has one or two ideas and you can call on players to expand on concepts that are addressed.

Explain the purpose of creating a common team mission that they will all contribute to. A good place to begin this discussion is by articulating some general team goals.

What do we want to achieve this year?

What are we willing to do to achieve this?

What types of compromises or sacrifices might we encounter as a team?

What will it take for this team to have a successful season?

Team cohesion is necessary for building strong communication skills, interactive play, and most of all, having fun!

strike, and it will, the coach must take the high road and remain positive and focused on the mission. This will show the players what is important and show them how overcoming adversity can, in fact, increase team cohesion.

Develop Integrity

Coaches should address integrity through direct communication. Integrity includes respect, honesty, and trust. In order to have integrity, a player must take personal responsibility for herself. She must represent her team in a manner that is recognized as highly commendable. When a team has a high level of integrity, the actions of all team members show how committed each member is to the team. To increase the integrity of their team, coaches should develop basic standards or requirements for player behavior—for example, establishing a minimum GPA requirement, a curfew on game nights, attitudes at practice, a dress code for travel, and a weight-training schedule. Coaches are encouraged to openly discuss each standard with the team. They should talk about the concept of pride and what it means to serve as a representative of your team, school, region, and state. The players should know that these requirements are not punitive but will be enforced to enhance the level of integrity and overall success of each team member both on and off the field.

Build Loyalty

Coaches must build loyalty among team members. Loyalty begins with establishing an identity—"I am a member of the Strike Zone softball team." But it takes more than group membership to develop loyalty. Nowadays, it is common to hear about players switching teams. If they are unhappy with their coach, are not getting enough playing time, or do not get along with their teammates, some players just quit and find another team. It happens every year, and some players even transfer schools during the middle of a season to move to a different team. If players do not stay on teams long enough to develop a relationship, continued success is difficult to sustain. Over time, teammates form special bonds that increase the enthusiasm and camaraderie that it takes to establish a cohesive unit. A player who is loyal is one who sticks with her team through good times and bad. Coaches can encourage a sense of loyalty by bringing the team together and reminding them to be proud of who they are and what they stand for—and also of what they will become. Coaches should validate the contributions of each player by acknowledging that what she does, whether on the bench or the field, provides an important contribution to the success of the team. Loyalty cannot be forced; it is derived from a connectedness with a group that produces a commitment similar to those experienced by families.

Define Roles

On softball teams, there are numerous roles that must be assumed. Furthermore, each team member is entitled to have a defined role. Role definition is a critical contributor to team cohesion.

One of the most common complaints players have about coaches is that they do not clearly define player roles on the team. It is important to differentiate between a player who doesn't know her role and a player who doesn't accept her role. However, coaches are often vague about role parameters. Many coaches presume that players understand their roles without explicit clarification. Coaches must be direct with players and convey the role that each player is expected to assume. Being truthful with all of the players can be difficult at times, especially when a player is not going to be happy with her assigned role. Coaches, in an attempt to be sensitive to player reactions, will sometimes beat around the bush to avoid hurting feelings. If a role is not addressed in a direct manner, the player will mentally struggle and constantly wonder what her coach is thinking. Eventually, she will realize that her role is not what she had hoped for, and this will hurt her more than if the coach would have told her in the first place. Not only does it hurt that she is not playing the role she prefers, but it also hurts to know that her coach didn't tell her directly. This may decrease her level of respect for the coach and may also lead to a negative attitude that will be detrimental to the team. Honesty is not always the easiest road, but if coaches want to maintain a good rapport with the players and a positive team environment, it is the only road worth navigating.

Unfortunately, only nine players can be on the field at one time. This means that some players will have to be on the bench, but it doesn't mean that their role should be minimized. Margo Jonker reiterated this point when she noted that "each player needs to be in the game." Clearly, she did not mean literally *in the game.* Coach Jonker meant that each team member has a specific role that must be performed in order to contribute to the team's success. The starters' roles are usually quite clear—there are certain hitting and fielding expectations. The bench players should also have meaningful roles that have an explicit purpose for the team. Those who do not play in the field have some of the most important roles. They provide their teammates with support and strategic information that could mean the difference between winning and losing. The roles of these players should be made public so they are noticed and appreciated by the team. Coaches should make it clear to everyone how each player is making her contribution and how this will propel the team in the direction of performance excellence. Without these bench players, the morale of the team, the intensity of practices, and the dynamics of team atmosphere would be entirely different. When a coach provides a definitive responsibility to each player and validates each player's contribution, she will develop an "attitude of service" to the team.

Player roles are discussed on page 176. Coaches who hold high expectations for all of their players are usually rewarded by outstanding individual efforts, and this leads to superior team performance.

Player Roles and Contributions

Discuss what athletes do to contribute to the team. Some roles that may emerge include batting, fielding, baserunning, tactics, team support, and attitude. It may be useful to generate a Player Role Form for each game outlining what is expected from each athlete.

To make the role specifications as concrete as possible, soccer expert Bill Beswick, in his book *Focused for Soccer: Develop a Winning Mental Approach,* suggests developing a job description for each position. The criteria used to determine who is the best fit for each role on the team should include assessing position needs, testing player ability, designing practices to improve specific physical and mental skills, and evaluating and rewarding improvement. Coaches should address roles in team meetings (instead of individual meetings) so that misinterpretations of role expectations do not undermine team chemistry.

The role of team captain is an important one. Some teams have captains and other teams do not. If used appropriately, captains can provide an effective line of communication between coaches and players. Although the position of captain is a significant one, many coaches are minimally involved in the selection process. For instance, several Division I intercollegiate head coaches reported that they simply let the team decide who should lead. This approach is difficult to understand considering the control many of these same coaches exert over their teams. Because captains are the coach's major link to the players, coaches should be involved in the process of assigning team captains. Coaches know their players and therefore should be able to determine who would best serve in this capacity. To leave this important task solely to the athletes allows for a popularity contest to determine this pivotal position. Figure 10.3 offers four strategies for team captain selection.

Choose Quality Players

Veteran coaches know that the key to great team cohesion lies in the quality of players—and this does not refer to talent level. Building team cohesion begins with the recruiting or selection process. There are three key issues to consider when selecting players for a team. One, a coach must determine whether a potential player

Figure 10.3   Selecting Team Captains

Captains play a vital role on any sports team. There are many ways to select the players who will serve as team captains. Here are four options for coaches to consider:

Coach Decision

One method for selecting team captains is having the coaching staff select the player or players who will serve the team best. Coaches know their players and know the type of leadership that will build team chemistry and guide the team to success.

Player Decision

Coaches can give players the power to select the player or players who will serve as team captains. Giving players input in the decision-making process empowers them. Players may also be more willing to commit to the team captain when they have a say in the process.

Coach and Player Decision

Nominating and voting for team captains can be performed jointly by both the coaching staff and the players. Each member of the team can be issued one vote or can rank the nominated players who will then be elected to serve as team captains.

Coach and Player Decision (Weighted Votes)

Another option that allows all team members, including coaches and players, to elect team captains involves a weighting system. In this system, the votes of coaches and players are weighted differently. Players' votes are weighted on a scale that gives more power to the more experienced players. For example, a vote cast by a senior counts as 1, juniors as .85, sophomores as .70, and freshmen as .50. Coaches' votes can be weighted as well—the head coach's vote can be weighted as 1.50, and the assistant coaches' votes as 1.25. If the team is not affiliated with a school, seniority can be determined by the number of years each member has played on the team. This gives everyone a vote, but the weighting system offers more power to those with more experience and status.

---

has good character. When Division I head coaches were asked how they ensure team chemistry, the overwhelming majority noted that a student-athlete's character is of prime importance. Two, a coach must try to assess whether the potential athlete will be a good team player. Remember the saying, "There is no 'I' in *team*." Does the player put the team ahead of her own needs and interests? Three, a coach should keep in mind that a mix of personality types will balance a team. Coach Teresa Wilson suggests that having a diverse group of players allows for different types of leaders, such as "vocal leaders, leaders by example, feisty players, calm players, good mom/sister figures, listeners, regulators, motivators, stabilizers, and even one or two instigators." An array of different personalities will allow for the development of leadership roles beyond the formal declaration of team captains, giving all of the players a unique status on the team.

Show Concern for Players

Showing concern for players is another factor that can directly influence team cohesion. The coach's expression of concern and care for the players must be genuine. Most coaches know their players very well as athletes, but a good way to show concern is to get to know them as people on and off the field. How many siblings do they have? What are their career goals? What is their favorite movie or book? Inquiring about each athlete as a person shows a genuine form of caring that facilitates cohesion on the team.

Treat Players Equitably

Coaches tend to treat players differently based on their skill levels. The better players are often given more feedback and better quality feedback. Players usually recognize this, and may consequently become resentful. This will damage team cohesion. Although equal treatment is unrealistic because every player has different needs, equitable treatment should be a goal. This means that all players are provided with a comparable amount of instruction and encouragement to continue improving. Using equitable feedback also recognizes all team members as necessary pieces in the complex puzzle of the team.

Ensure Consistency on the Coaching Staff

A final means for building cohesion involves the coaching staff. Coaches should train their assistants in the philosophy they endorse. On most teams, there are more assistant than head coaches. Furthermore, players often view assistant coaches as more approachable than the head coach. Thus, it is imperative that the assistant coaches buy into the head coach's philosophy of team building. If an assistant coach conducts a drill or teaches a technique that is not consistent with the head coach's vision, the head coach should address this issue with the assistant coach privately so that the assistant maintains the respect of the players. This is part of the learning process, and it will ensure a positive working relationship among the coaching staff. If a group of 3 or 4 coaches is unable to work together as a staff, they cannot expect a group of 15 to 20 players to work together as a team. Consistency among the coaching staff will reinforce to the players that everyone is on the same page and is striving to meet the same team mission.

It is not enough to just build cohesion. Once strong levels of cohesion exist on a team, the coach must work to sustain that cohesion because it will be tested throughout a season. A coach shouldn't get too comfortable with the existing level of team bonding because there will be times when the players get disappointed and frustrated, and forget the team mission. To maintain a strong sense of cohesion, coaches must continue to reinforce the central components of cohesion as defined on their team. Issues that might undermine team cohesion should be discussed during team meetings. In these sessions, the coach should encourage open dialogue among the players providing a safe environment where they will not be ostracized or judged. The coach should stress that the identity of the team hinges on the connectedness of all members. This might also be a good opportunity for the coach to remind players of their team roles and how those roles are essential for performance excellence.

TEAM-BUILDING ACTIVITIES

Increasing team cohesion clearly has the potential to directly affect performance. This chapter provides concrete strategies for coaches to consider as they strive to boost team chemistry. Figure 10.4 offers additional team-building exercises that can be used any time throughout the softball season. These activities will allow players to learn more about each other and to practice their communication skills. This will foster an environment where players can connect as a team both on and off the field.

Figure 10.4 Activity Cards

My Personality

Instructions: Give each player a notecard and pen. Instruct the players to write down three statements about themselves that nobody else on the team knows. When each player is finished, collect the notecards. Read some of the cards, and ask the players to guess who wrote each one.

(continued)

Figure 10.4 (continued)

Sample card

> **I never**...ride roller coasters.
> **I always**...listen to rock music.
> **Personality trait**...I get frustrated easily.

If I Only Knew

Instructions: Give each player two notecards and a pen. Instruct the players to write down one question that they would like their teammates to answer. Collect the first set of notecards and read through them to find interesting questions. Read aloud one question at a time, and have players write their answers on the second notecard. After asking 5 to 10 questions, have the players share their response to each question.

Sample Questions

What is your biggest fear?

If you could only eat one type of food, what would it be? Why?

If you could change one thing about your life, what would you change?

What Would You Do If?

Instructions: Give each player a notecard and a pen. Instruct the players to compose a creative question that begins with this statement: What would you do if . . . ? Collect the notecards and randomly redistribute them to the team. Team members will take turns responding to the question on their new notecard.

Sample Questions

What would you do if you knew you wouldn't fail?

What would you do if an umpire called you safe, but you knew that you were out?

What would you do if your coach told you to do something that was against your principles?

Game Review

This activity is most beneficial after a game or tournament. Give each player a notecard and pen. Instruct the players to write one positive and specific thought about the game or tournament. Collect the notecards and anonymously read the statements to the team. This activity is a good avenue to enhance communication and facilitate team discussion.

Where Am I? Where Are You?

Instructions: This activity should be performed on the field or an area where players can safely roam around blindfolded. Every player gets a blindfold. Ask the team to organize themselves into groups based on certain characteristics. Do not allow the players to use any verbal comments or noises while forming groups. The ultimate challenge is for players to develop unique and creative modes of communication.

For example, ask players to organize themselves by the following:

Position (infield/outfield)	Birth month
Age	Sibling order
Year in school	Favorite color
Shoe size	Favorite music

Encouraging Words

Instructions: Give each player a notecard and a pen. Instruct each player to write her name on the top of the notecard. Collect all of the notecards and randomly redistribute them to the team. Instruct the players to write down a nice comment about the person whose name is on their notecard. Collect all of the notecards and randomly redistribute them for a second time. Finally, the players should take turns reading the name of the player and the comment about the player on their notecard. Return the notecard to the person who originally wrote her name on the card.

Getting to Know You

Instruct the team to form a circle. The coach will ask questions designed to help players find out what they have in common. You can use any type of question that will get team members to become more familiar with each other. Those players who respond affirmatively to the questions go to the middle of the circle; these players must find one additional commonality and one difference, and then report these to the group before leaving the middle of the circle.

Sample Questions

Who was born in September?

Who has a pet at home?

Who likes to go camping?

Who wears a size eight and a half shoe?

Who has a twin?

Whose favorite fruit is bananas?

Who has traveled outside the United States?

Who has coached children?

BIBLIOGRAPHY

Beswick, B. 2001. *Focused for Soccer: Develop a Winning Mental Approach.* Champaign, IL: Human Kinetics.

Janssen, J. 1999. *Championship Team Building.* Tucson, AZ: Winning the Mental Game Publishers.

Jonker, M. 2002. "Making softball fun." In *The Softball Coaching Bible,* ed. J. Joseph, 9-20. Champaign, IL: Human Kinetics.

Joseph, J. 1998. *Defensive Softball Drills.* Champaign, IL: Human Kinetics.

Orlick, T. 2000. *In Pursuit of Excellence: How to Win in Sport and Life Through Mental Training.* 3rd ed. Champaign, IL: Human Kinetics.

Solomon, G.B. 2002. Performance and personality impression cues as predictors of athletic performance: An extension of expectancy theory. *International Journal of Sport Psychology* 32:88-100.

Solomon, G.B. 2002. Sources of expectancy information among assistant coaches: The influence of performance and psychological cues. *Journal of Sport Behavior* 25:279-286.

Solomon, G.B. and D.J. Rhea. (In review). Sources of expectancy information among college coaches: A qualitative test of expectancy theory.

Solomon, G.B., D.A. Striegel, J.F. Eliot, S.N. Heon, J.L. Maas, and V.K. Wayda. 1996. The self-fulfilling prophecy in college basketball: Implications for effective coaching. *Journal of Applied Sport Psychology* 8:44-59.

Wilson, T. 2002. Outhustling your opponent. In *The Softball Coaching Bible,* ed. J. Joseph, 33-40. Champaign, IL: Human Kinetics.

ABOUT THE AUTHORS

Gloria Solomon, PhD, is an assistant professor of kinesiology at California State University at Sacramento. She is a certified AAASP sport psychology consultant and serves as a consultant for the Sacramento State athletic department. She has been working as team consultant for the softball team for two years. Solomon currently resides in Sacramento, California, and in her free time she enjoys kayaking, running, reading, and supporting the Sacramento Monarchs.

Photo courtesy of Dr. Gloria Solomon

Andrea Becker is a graduate student of sport psychology at California State University at Sacramento. Becker played softball at CSUS for four seasons and has since served as a graduate assistant coach and sport psychology intern for the softball program. In addition, she has numerous playing and coaching experiences at various levels of competition in the Amateur Softball Association summer leagues. Becker resides in Folsom, California, and enjoys watching and participating in sports and all other outdoor activities.

Photo courtesy of Andrea Becker

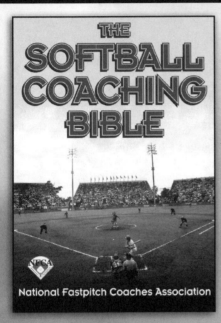